ALSO BY W. TIMOTHY GALLWEY

The Inner Game of Tennis

INNER TENNIS
Playing the Game

INNER TENNIS
Playing the Game

W. TIMOTHY GALLWEY

RANDOM HOUSE
NEW YORK

Library of Congress Cataloging in Publication Data

Gallwey, W   Timothy.
    Inner tennis.

    I. Tennis. I. Title.
GV995.G28   796.34'22   76–14199
        ISBN 0–394–40043–7

Manufactured in the United States of America

2 4 6 8 9 7 5 3

FIRST EDITION

To my wife, Sally,
and to all those like her who seek
to connect with the source of their lives

and to
Guru Maharaj Ji,
who for me has made that connection
a practical possibility

You have it in your power
to conquer the ego and doubts of the mind.

—Guru Maharaj Ji

Contents

1
The Inner Game: An Introduction to Basic Principles   *3*

2
Leaving Your Mind and Coming to Your Senses   *26*

3
Overcoming Boredom   *47*

4
Feeling the Difference: An Introduction to Body
          Awareness   *71*

5
Ways of Cooperating with Natural Learning in Tennis   *88*

6
Self-Image   *111*

7
The Will to Win   *137*

8
On Winning the Inner Game   *170*

INNER TENNIS
Playing the Game

1
The Inner Game:
An Introduction to
Basic Principles

A tennis player first confronts the Inner Game when he discovers that there is an opponent inside his own head more formidable than the one across the net. He then realizes that the greatest difficulty in returning a deep backhand lies not in the speed and placement of the ball itself, but in his mind's reaction to that ball: his own thinking makes the shot more difficult than it really is. Further, he becomes aware that these same mental obstacles which keep him from playing his best tennis also prevent him from living his best life.

If, for example, while the tennis ball is approaching (non-tennis players may take the ball as a metaphor for any event entering their experience), your mind is screaming, "You're probably going to miss this one just like the last one . . . You'd better get your racket back earlier and make sure to meet the ball out front . . . Remember to keep your wrist firm, and don't forget to follow through . . . If I miss, I'll be down 5–3 on his serve . . . I doubt if I can last a third set . . . What will they think back at the club when they found I lost my challenge match to Jim?"—if thoughts like these are occupying the mind, the ball will appear to approach much faster than it actually is and will not be seen clearly, and your stroke will be too tight and too contrived to be either effective or fun. In short, when one's mind is disturbed by anxiety, self-doubt and concern about one's image, and consequently is overfilled with instructions, self-criticisms and thoughts about future and past, it prohibits the full expression of one's potential at that instant. This is true whether the participant is hitting a tennis ball, making a speech, taking an exam, making a business decision or is involved in any other activity.

Understanding that errors in performance usually take place in his mind before they express themselves in his actions, the player of the Inner Game sets as his primary goal the overcoming of the mental obstacles that prevent his best performance. He recognizes that his full potential already exists within himself, and that his first objective at every succeeding level of excellence is to rid himself of the still-remaining mental limitations which prevent its total expression. He stops thinking that another person or external event —such as losing a match—can prevent him from reaching his goal. He begins to realize that his only real obstacles in life are self-imposed, and that their removal—and *only* their removal—will allow him to enjoy and express his true capabilities.

Experience has shown me that because of the interference from our own minds we come to know only a very small portion of our human potential. The aim of the Inner Game approach is to help the player of life to get in touch with the already self-existing process that I call "natural learning." This process has always guided the evolution and development of all aspects of our lives, and we must cooperate with its intention in order to know and express fully our human potentiality. Natural learning can be explored by the player of the Inner Game in an unlimited variety of external situations or activities. No matter what the *outer* game, the inner game remains the same, so whatever is learned in exploring it can immediately become useful in *all* outer games. If a player learns a new technique for hitting a serve, he will only be able to use that skill on the tennis court, but if at the same time he also learns how to increase his power of concentration, that inner skill can influence the quality of his entire life. He will use this power of concentration while playing golf, doing business, solving a problem, relating to another person and pursuing any other purpose.

What are some of the inner obstacles which prevent us from doing our best? Here is a partial list of mental difficulties reported by tennis players whom I have taught. Note that the list is remarkably similar to one which could be compiled on any activity or subject.

1. Fear

fear of losing, of not improving, of not playing well;

fear of looking bad in the eyes of others;

fear of losing one's self-esteem;

fear (by women) of beating men, or (by men) of losing to women;

fear of not being accepted by one's group, of not being asked to play again;

fear of being hit by a ball;

fear of making errors;

fear of not meeting expectations—those of self or of others;

choking on crucial points, in tournaments, etc.;

fear of missing easy shots.

2. Lack of self-confidence

"I don't believe in myself."

"I have low self-esteem."

"I consider myself a loser."

"I trust myself on some shots, but I lose confidence in my backhand (volley, serve, etc.)."

3. Self-condemnation

"I get down on myself."

"I'm always judging my shots."

"I get angry at myself and self-critical."

4. Poor concentration

distraction ("My mind wanders easily to other things.")

duration ("I can't sustain concentration for long. There are large intervals between short periods of concentration.")

depth (I seldom become deeply concentrated; I stay on the surface, never really growing absorbed.")

5. Trying too hard

("I always try hard, but the harder I try the worse I seem to get. I strain and get too tight. I have difficulty relaxing.")

6. *Lack of will to win*
   "I just don't have the killer instinct."
   "I get ahead 5–1, then blow the match."
   "I have a hard time really getting up for a match."
   "I seldom put out my full effort. I play half-heartedly."
   "I can't sustain my dedication to reaching my goals."

7. *Perfectionism*
   "I'm never content unless I'm perfect—and I'm never perfect."
   "I never let myself feel good about the progress I make because it never seems good enough."

8. *Self-consciousness*
   "I'm constantly thinking about how well or badly I'm playing, or about how I look."

9. *Frustration*
   "After I miss a few, I become so frustrated that I get angry or feel like quitting."

10. *Anger*
    at myself;
    at my opponent;
    at my husband for giving me advice (and those critical looks);
    at my pro;
    at referees, linesmen and ball boys;
    at luck, which usually favors my opponents;
    at the wind.

11. *Boredom*
    "I just don't have much fun playing."
    "I work hard, but don't enjoy practicing."
    "I can't sustain my interest in the game any more."

12. *Expectations*
    "I place too high expectations on myself."
    "I don't expect enough of myself."
    "Others expect too much of me."
    "Others don't expect enough of me."
    "I don't have a good self-image."

13. *A busy mind*
    "My mind is so busy telling me what I should do with my feet, arms, wrist, elbows, etc., that I miss the ball."

This list of mental obstacles may seem discouragingly long, but the principles of solution are few and simple, though they may not always seem easy to practice. Many people who read my first book, *The Inner Game of Tennis,* which presented my initial insights into these principles, found that their games underwent dramatic improvement almost immediately, and that they could apply what they had learned to many aspects of their lives. But some also found this initial rate of progress difficult to sustain and fell back into old mental habits—or developed new ways of interfering with themselves. For example, instead of trying hard as they had in the past to follow the right technique for hitting a running forehand, now they were trying to "let go," or straining to concentrate. As a result, they judged themselves for not playing the Inner Game well—or just for being judgmental! In short, they met old enemies in new, more subtle disguises.

Lasting progress in the Inner Game requires more than inspiration and understanding; it also requires practical methods. In the remaining pages of this chapter I will summarize and clarify the principles presented in *The Inner Game of Tennis,* and then, in the following chapters, emphasize the methods and techniques that I have found helpful in sustaining progress in my own Inner Game and those of my students. Ultimately, Inner Game training is a proper balance between understanding, inspiration and practical methods, and it can produce success in any game—or even in choosing a game worth playing.

The Fundamentals of the Inner Game of Tennis

Self 1 and Self 2

Most tennis players who take a moment to listen to what is going on inside their heads will discover an almost interminable conversation which stops only in rare periods of intent concentration. The rest of the time this dialogue drones on, reminding you to watch the ball, how to hit it, what might happen if you miss, and so forth.

As each individual listens to the conversation in his mind, he can begin to understand a little about what is preventing him from playing his best. If he hears "C'mon, stupid, when are you going to remember to meet the ball in front," or "Dammit, there you go again, not getting sideways—no wonder you're lousy," or "I'm not very steady—I hope he misses soon, because if he doesn't I will," the chances are his problems have more to do with his relation to himself than with his ability to play tennis.

Listening to Your Internal Dialogue

By listening to your internal dialogue objectively, you can get an idea of who is talking to whom. Wherever there is a conversation, there must be more than one present. Communication always means there are at least two entities; otherwise, there would be no need to communicate. So listen to the voice which is doing the talking and see what it's like. Who is it talking to, and how does that self get along with the other self? Imagine what kind of relationship they would have if they were two separate people outside your own head. With most players, the self doing the talking seems to know all about how to play tennis because it is telling the other self —the part that actually has to hit the ball—how to do it. By the tone of this instructional voice—Self 1—and the names it calls Self 2, it's easy to tell that there is not a great sense of trust between them. There is often so much mistrust between these two that Self 1 not only repeats endlessly the same command ("Racket back early . . . Racket back early . . . Racket back early"), showing that it thinks Self 2 has a very short memory, but even feels it necessary to instruct the arm *how* to take itself back. Then, having told it how, Self 1 doesn't trust that the arm will do it right because it is a "bad" arm, with a "bad" habit, so it *makes* the arm do it correctly, tightening most of the muscles in the arm (and face!) as it tries to force it into Self 1's idea of the right position. Being too tight to make a smooth and accurate connection with the ball, the arm misguides the racket, the ball is mis-hit and

Self 1 calls Self 2 still one more degrading name. The mistrust continues, so does the tightness, and so do the errors.

The more Self 1 mistrusts Self 2, the more it worries; the more it worries, the more it feels it has to instruct the body on what to do and the more it has to "try hard" to make it happen. The harder Self 1 tries, the tighter it gets and the worse it plays. The discouragement and frustration that follow take the fun out of the game—proficiency already having departed.

Trust Your Body

The first principle of Inner Game learning is to trust your body. Trust Self 2. The capacity of the human body to learn on its own, without the help of all the verbal self-instructions and self-doubts, is immeasurably greater than we imagine. Only when we succeed in quieting Self 1—the conscious, thinking, egoistic mind—does the true potential of the human body begin to show itself. Uninterfered with, Self 2 shows a talent so great that we are often afraid even to identify with it, so far is it beyond our normal expectations. When it produces a shot that flies off the racket, undistorted by our own "trying," we stand amazed and call it lucky. Sometimes we feel as if someone else hit the shot. Yet if we don't immediately become self-conscious about this phenomenon, we can repeat it over and over—until Self 1 comes rushing back to try to analyze what's causing us to play so well, so that it can make it happen some more. When it starts trying, you start missing, the magic is broken, and you are left only with some wonderful memories which others won't believe. Soon you will begin to doubt yourself again.

In any sport a common expression for this type of play is "playing out of one's mind," or "over one's head." Both Arthur Ashe and Billie Jean King used this phrase to describe their performances while winning the finals at Wimbledon in 1975. In Inner Game terms it means a momentary disappearance of Self 1 and, thus, no interference from conscious thought. The player loses himself in the action, continually breaking the false limits placed on his potential. Awareness becomes acutely heightened, while analysis, anxiety and self-conscious thought are completely forgotten. Enjoyment is at a peak—pure and unspoiled. The inherent rewards of these experiences of peak performance are so great that attaining any external goal seems unnecessary, even superfluous. If only I could keep out of my mind, the player finds himself thinking. Once out of the experience, the greatest desire is to get back into it.

Natural Learning

Hence, the first skill needed for the Inner Game is called "letting it happen." This means gradually building a trust in the innate ability of your own body to learn and to perform. Building this relationship of trust takes a little time, but it can start immediately. Instead of telling your body what to do, let it do what it wants to, let it have its way. Don't scold it for its mistakes, but let it learn from them. Let your body control itself without any henpecking from your mind. Anyone who does this rediscovers natural learning, the beautiful process by which we learned how to walk and talk.

Watch a child learn—there is natural intelligence showing itself to anyone who stops to see it. By this process the child learns and grows more in his first five years than he is likely to during the rest of his life. Watch a baby learn to swim—without a word of instruction. Watch a five-year-old learn skiing quickly, naturally, joyously, competently, simply by watching and doing. See him absorb what he needs to learn from each new experience thoughtlessly, yet intelligently. Let a small baby hold on to your finger and you will experience one of the most efficient uses of available strength possible; yet there is no straining, no "trying." The hand does not seem controlled from the part of his mind which gives verbal instructions; it is a silent, wordless order which tells him when to grasp and when to let go. Both joy and intelligence are instructing him.

Imagine a child learning to walk falling over to the right and thinking to himself, Dammit, I fell to the right again. I think I let my head tilt to the right and lost my balance. I've got to remember to keep my head straight. It's sure taking me a long time to learn to walk; I wish I were as coordinated as Jimmy—he's younger and already walking. Oh well, I'll keep trying. Now, step out, plant the heel, roll to the ball of the foot, shift and step out with the other—and don't forget to keep your head straight! If we had been thinking like this while learning to walk, we'd still be tripping now and then, just as we do in tennis when we try to instruct ourselves on the right footwork in the middle of a point. But by the grace of the Almighty, as children we learned how to walk before we learned how to talk, so that no parent or teacher could put ideas in our minds about the right and wrong styles, or make us aware of our progress relative to others. Consequently, we didn't experience self-condemnation or take credit for doing well. We were not concerned with our self-image, and so our energy went into growing and learning instead of trying to live up to the expectations of others. Falling was not a bad event; it was just a little surprising and perhaps a little painful. But though we did not think about how to correct our mistake, we still learned from our experiences and therefore quickly outgrew this failing. In all physical movements we tended only to use the muscles necessary, so we did not overtighten. Our relative weakness did not bother us; we were content to be where we were, yet made great effort to grow and to learn. We could see, feel, hear, smell and taste without the interruption of interpretive thought. We experienced life more directly and were less separated from our innate intelligence. We came, in Wordsworth's words, "trailing clouds of glory . . ." This was true of all of us; in childhood we were each that spontaneous.

As adults, however, we have largely forgotten the natural process that taught us in the early years to walk, talk and learn about life. Filled with concerns about our self-image, we call ourselves stupid and uncoordinated whenever we fail to live up to expectations—and soon we begin to act stupid and uncoordinated. But we can gradually recapture the effectiveness of natural learning by simply recognizing that it is still operative in us. Even now we learn more by direct experience than by trying to master concepts *about* experience. We learn more by seeing someone play good tennis than by reading a book about how to play good tennis. Trying to force one's body into the mold of concepts taken from an external source is a long and frustrating process.

Even so, learning eventually takes place because experience is always there to teach us and eventually manages to get its messages across in spite of the interference of a mind full of concepts of right and wrong. But if instead of just watching a tennis player "emptily" as a child would, you analyze his every move, thinking, Oh, I see, he swings his forehand in a loop, keeps his elbow in close to his body, lifts up as he hits, and so on, when you get out on the court you will be as deliberate and awkward as if you were trying to put into practice a whole set of instructions from a book. The idea is to watch with an open and quiet mind. Watch so attentively that you can "feel" the player's movements, and when you go out to play don't try to imitate. Then your game will definitely show the effects of watching the better player, but perhaps in ways of which you are not even aware. You may find yourself playing better without knowing why. Most people experience this phenomenon after watching a tournament when they made no effort to pick up any tips. They are surprised at how much better they play the next day, and only afterwards do they realize that it must have had something to do with watching the matches the day before. (Note: If you happen to realize what you are doing differently, it won't hurt, but if you then try to mentally enforce those concepts on your body, you will again start getting in your own way.)

I know a mother who loves to observe her child learn and grow. When her daughter was at the stage between walking and running, this mother used to take her to a park where many children of all ages played. She told me that she would observe her daughter watching the other children, and notice that she didn't look at the one-year-olds who were just toddling; nor was she much interested in the older children who were running easily. Instead she concentrated on the children who were just a little more progressed than she and could teach her what she needed to know. Did she have to be told that she could learn by observing, and just whom to observe? Was she analyzing or feeling envious? No, she was experiencing pure, relaxed concentration, in perfect harmony with her Self 2 and with no interference from Self 1. Very beautiful.

The Inner Game suggests that this same intelligence is still at work within us, and that it can learn and play better tennis than "we" can. All we need to do is learn to trust it, to quiet our minds, and to stop trying so hard.

Trying versus Effort

Some people who read *The Inner Game of Tennis* found the concept of not trying hard a difficult, even disturbing one. Doesn't it take a lot of effort to play tennis or learn any other skill? Doesn't success in anything depend on how hard you try? This is an understandable and important question for the player of the Inner Game to confront because in our culture we have been repeatedly told, "If at first you don't succeed, try, try, again." We value trying hard highly and believe that whatever deficiencies we have as a people or as a culture can be overcome by trying. Still, we also know from experience that often when we are trying our hardest we perform the poorest. We also recognize that when we just let go and "let it happen" we are at our best. There seems to be a contradiction. When I'm trying hard, I seem to be too tight, too serious, too calculated, but if I relax too much, I doubt that I will accomplish anything, much less improve.

To distinguish conceptually between trying too hard and putting in just the necessary amount of effort is difficult, but it is easy to experience the difference, especially in a physical activity such as tennis.

First let's try it conceptually. It does take *effort* to run across the court and hit a tennis ball, but it does not take *trying*. It takes effort for the baby to learn to walk or grasp your finger, but not trying. "Trying" is a word I use for Self 1 effort. It is born of self-doubt, and is usually characterized by a lot of self-instruction and self-conscious effort to make up for imagined deficiencies. It is Self 1 "helping" a mistrusted Self 2 because it doubts its potential. But we don't *try* to walk, talk or drive a car because we trust ourselves in these activities and just do them. We don't tell our bodies, "Put your foot on the brake and stop at the intersection. Now shift into first and turn the wheel clockwise to make this right turn." If because of self-doubt we "tried hard" while driving, we would interfere with our true capacity and would greatly increase our chances of having an accident. Most people drive along having a conversation with a companion, listening to a radio and perhaps doing two or three other things; yet they still halt at stop signs, make turns and end up at their destination, having successfully and calmly avoided many opportunities to kill themselves. It's really quite automatic.

But did it take effort? Yes, of course. "Effort" is the word I use for Self 2 exertion. Left on its own, the human body makes an effort to perform an action, but only the amount necessary to complete it. There is no *extra* effort, no Self 1 motivation, and therefore no sense of trying too hard; consequently, it seems easy. Zen masters sometimes call this mode of doing "effortless effort," which is a hard phrase to understand. But then, it is hard for Self 1 to understand why it is not needed, and to understand how easy Self 2 effort really is.

The Unbendable Arm Demonstration. Experiencing the difference between Self 1 "trying" and Self 2 "effort" is easier than trying to understand it through any abstract explanation.

Try this experiment, a demonstration often used by aikido teachers to explain "effortless effort." Ask someone of equal or greater strength to test the strength of your arm by placing one of his or her hands on your biceps just above the elbow and the other hand on your wrist. Then ask this person to apply enough pressure to bend your arm at the elbow. Try really hard to keep your elbow from bending, and while keeping your arm strong, count out loud to five. Then ask your partner to gauge how difficult it was to bend your arm —or if it didn't bend, gauge how long you could have held out before your arm bent. This first half of the experiment could be called "trying hard to be strong."

Now shake any tension out of your arm, relax it and raise it again. This time as your partner grabs hold, don't try so hard to keep it straight; in fact, don't try at all. Simply ask your arm to keep itself straight; let it do the best it can without any help from you. If you like, you can observe objectively the strength of your arm, but don't try to add to it. If you want to occupy your mind, simply imagine that you are using your partner's strength against him to keep your arm from bending. Then ask your partner to slowly apply pressure up to the same level as before, and then beyond.

When he is applying more pressure than before, count out loud again to five. Is your voice relaxed? If you really let your arm keep *itself* strong, your partner will find it considerably more difficult to bend, and you will have the sense that you could keep it strong for a much longer period of time. More strength and less trying. It almost seems like magic, and you may wonder if your partner was really applying as much pressure.

But it's not magic; the explanation is only embarrassing. Put your arm out again in the first position, the mode of "trying hard." Are all your fingers clenched tight? Your forearm? Your biceps? Your cheeks? Your other cheeks? Your throat? Count out loud to five. Is your voice tight and constrained? If your answers to these questions were all "yes," you really were trying hard.

The embarrassing part of the explanation is that the above is an intelligence test flunked miserably by Self 1, who pretends to know so much about the body that it tells it what to do and not to do. Was it really necessary to keep the fingers tight to keep the elbow from bending? Your forearm? Your cheeks and your throat muscles? Of course, none of those muscles were functional in keeping the elbow straight. What you spent in energy was a lot of extra trying. Self 1's way of making *sure* that the arm is strong is to tighten everything. That's not smart—and it's also very tiring. Now consider what happens when you tighten your biceps. Try it. Relax all muscles but the biceps. What happens? Your elbow bends! The function of the biceps is to bend the elbow— exactly the *opposite* of your supposed intention. That's not just stupid, it's sabotage! Self 1 is working directly against your purpose. All that sweating and straining to work against yourself! Embarrassing, perhaps, but true.

Now take the second position, the mode of letting your arm keep itself strong. Feel your forearm and biceps with your opposite hand. Are they soft or hard? Then count out loud to five. Is your throat tight or relaxed? All these muscles can be relaxed while your arm remains strong against any pressure to bend it. Next, relax the arm and see how easy it is to bend; in fact, it won't even stay raised if you relax completely. So keeping the arm straight requires *some* muscles, but not many. Which ones did you tighten to keep it straight? You probably don't know, but *something—*Self 2—

did. Of course, Self 1 can learn that there are certain extensor muscles which will keep the arm strong, and can feel that he is really in control by telling his body, "Tighten the extensors and keep them tight until I say let go!" But is this really necessary?

What does all this have to do with tennis? Who really knows how to play tennis? Who learns, and from whom? Ask a playing professional how he wrote his book. The chances are that he picked up his racket, swung a few forehands, looked down at his grip and then described it in a paragraph on the forehand grip. You'll find that pros who write down their concepts of how tennis *should* be played seldom actually play that way. The mind learns from the body. Unfortunately, it then often uses this knowledge *against* the body so that it can play the role of teacher instead of student. Therefore, when my mind gets a little arrogant about its so-called knowledge of how to play tennis (I once made a list of approximately one hundred different instructions for hitting a correct forehand), I ask it some simple questions like these: "Okay, if you know everything about how to hit a forehand, would you tell me how you get your racket moving once you're in the ready position?" I can't answer. "And once it has started moving back, how do you get it to change direction and start swinging forward? Do you tell it to?" Of course not. It would be impossible to run across a court and hit a ball if you were directing all the bodily movements. So why pretend? It's your body that has to learn to play, and once it *has* learned, it's your body that plays! It will make the necessary effort within its developed capacities in a natural, sophisticated way if you allow it to. What it needs is not a doubting concept-filled mind, but an alert and concentrated one.

If your Self 1 needs more convincing, look at animals in action. You don't see many uncoordinated birds flying across the sky. The leopard isn't thinking about technique at the moment that he's about to jump upon his prey. There is no self-doubt, no trying, and consequently no uncoordination, because no Self 1 is on hand to worry about its image. There is no mind-body split, simply pure spontaneous action, with a lot of learning in failure as well as in success. Just imagine playing the net with the concentration and quickness of a cat reaching for flies!

Satisfying Self 1 versus Satisfying Self 2

You would think that playing "out of your mind" and letting your body express its own excellence would be a clearly preferable way to perform most actions. But not all people find the choice between Self 1 and Self 2 control a simple one. Self 1 often misses the sense of its control and achieving the sense of credit and self-importance which comes when it feels it's in charge. As the mind quiets, ego satisfaction departs, and though another kind of satisfaction replaces it, each individual chooses for himself. When Billie Jean King beat Evonne Goolagong 6–0, 6–1, at Wimbledon, playing "out of her mind" what she termed the best tennis of her life, she spoke of the resulting satisfaction afterwards: "I felt so good because I felt I totally expressed myself. I got all that was in me out. I felt sorry for Evonne, but I really couldn't help it." That is a beautiful statement of what it's all about: "to get all that is within you out." It means simply to completely fulfill your potential. Whenever we do this, we have a wonderful feeling of nearing completion. But another kind of satisfaction, that of the ego, is missing from such an experience, and some players find the absence of this sense of Self 1 achievement a loss, even a kind of "death." As Self 1 control is replaced by that of Self 2, Self 2's satisfaction replaces Self 1's ego-satisfaction, and at first this choice may not be easy.

I remember a lawyer who came for an Inner Game lesson on his serve. "I want more power," he said.

"Serve a few."

As he set himself in position, his hand gripped his racket handle like a vise, and his shoulders, forearms and biceps were tight almost to the point of shaking. His thighs bulged, and his cheeks and jaw were locked with determination. Five strained but weak serves followed, only one of which landed in the court.

"Was there any power?" I asked.

"No! None. I was trying hard, but I don't know how to get more power. How am I supposed to do it?"

"Ask your body for power, but don't try to produce it yourself."

Three serves. Much freer movement. About 10 percent of his muscles had relaxed.

"More power," said the lawyer, a little surprised, but without much enthusiasm.

"Let go a little more. Simply let your body serve the ball without any help from you and see what happens."

After about three minutes of silent serving, the speed of the lawyer's serve had doubled.

"How am I doing that?"

"Your body did it."

"Oh."

Three more serves, the freest yet. Only about 50 percent of his muscles were tight.

"What am I doing differently?"

"A lot of things. Keep letting go a little more with each serve."

Within ten minutes the lawyer's wrist was loose enough to snap through the ball, and there was a *crack* instead of a *plop* singing from his strings. His face was relaxed as he kept serving, saying nothing.

"How does it feel?"

"A lot easier. A lot easier. It's hard to believe."

But there was still little enthusiasm in his voice. *Either he's very cool, or he's concerned that not enough of his balls are going in,* I thought to myself. "You want more accuracy," I say.

"Yeah, that would help. How can I keep it in the court?"

"See that backhand corner?"

"Yeah."

"Ask your body to hit the ball into it. Don't try. Let the body learn how to do it without any help from you. Just see where the ball goes."

He served. "About three feet wide and two feet long."

"Now, don't try to correct. Let the body serve again and see where the ball goes this time."

"Further to the left."

"How much?"

"About three more feet."

"Again. No correction—just let it happen, and notice where the ball lands."

"In the corner."

Ten minutes later the lawyer was hitting either corner at will within two feet of his target. I was amazed; I always am to see how naturally and efficiently the body can learn when it is not interfered with.

The lawyer thanked me cordially and walked off the court. Then he turned around and came back.

"How about another lesson next week on the backhand?"

"Fine."

Next week I asked the lawyer how he had played in the meantime.

"Oh, pretty good, I guess."

"What do you want to do today?"

"I think I'd like to work on my backhand. I do a lot of things wrong."

"Okay, but how about serving a few for me first? I'm curious to see how it's doing after a week."

He agreed, and then proceeded to serve five floaters, every one of his muscles straining—exact replicas of his serves at the beginning of the lesson the week before. But though only two landed in the court, there was no expression of dissatisfaction from the lawyer. Without asking for any comments, he said matter-of-factly, "Okay? Now, let's start with the backhand."

I was astonished. *Either this lawyer became enlightened during the week, or something else is happening.* "Okay, but tell me what happened to the serve you found last week?"

"Oh, that," the lawyer exclaimed as if his memory of a year-old event had been jarred. "Well, to tell you the truth, I have to admit that I really didn't like that serve much. I know that it was quite a bit faster and was accurate, but I didn't seem to have any control over it. I didn't feel I knew what I was doing. This serve may not be as strong or as accurate, but at least I know what I'm doing!"

There was nothing to say. It was the clearest verbal description of the choice which confronts the player of the Inner Game from the very beginning. Who is hitting the ball? Who is doing the action? Who is doing the learning? Who gets the credit? Am I willing to get out of my own way? How much control am I willing to surrender to a superior center of control within me? Who do I choose to be?

Quieting the Mind

Trusting the body is the first principle of the Inner Game of sports. The second is *quieting the mind.* The capacity of our bodies to perform at their highest potential is in direct proportion to the stillness of our minds. When the mind is noisy, anxious and distracted, it interferes with the nervous system's silent instructions to the muscles. It's like static in the communication system; the subtler messages get drowned out and there is little subtlety in the body's motion. If the static is at high volume, then even the most elementary messages get blocked out and we miss relatively easy shots.

Controlling and quieting Self 1 so that it pays attention to what is essential is the primary art of the Inner Game. As long as the mind is in control of the body, it will jerk you around spasmodically, following a million impulses and desires that catch its fancy. For Self 2 to regain control, so that you can say, "Mind, stay on the ball," and have it obey, some effort and practice are required. When this is achieved, the right relationship between Self 1 and Self 2 is established. Only then are you in charge of your mind, able to use it as a tool when it is needed, rather than letting it use you.

The art of quieting the mind is the central theme of the Inner Game and will be discussed in a practical way in following chapters. But first let us look at the relationship between our ability to learn and perform and the state of our minds.

Natural Learning: A Function of Awareness

There is no learning, no growth, no action, without awareness. Awareness is the basic element of all human activities. Whatever increases it increases one's learning potential, and whatever decreases it interferes with one's learning potential. This is the essence of Inner Game learning theory.

What is awareness? It is the energy of consciousness which

makes it possible for us to experience events internal or external to our bodies. Awareness is what makes it possible to experience a tennis ball through your sense of sight or feel. Without awareness you could experience neither, and therefore could neither hit the ball nor learn anything from hitting it. Though this may seem abstract, it is important to understand it. On a practical level there is only one way to progress in the Inner Game: *to increase awareness* of what is. Every method and technique in the remainder of this book will be designed to do nothing but to simply increase awareness of what already is. If you want to change your tennis—or your life—the Inner Game approach suggests that as a first step you *not* try to change it, but simply increase your awareness of the way it *is.*

Memory and Awareness

There would also be no learning without memory. If what you have experienced by virtue of being aware were not somehow recorded and stored, every time you saw a tennis ball coming it would seem as if it were for the first time. You would know nothing about where it was going to land; in fact, you wouldn't even expect it to fall, any more than you would expect it to rise endlessly, or to make loops. There would be no basis for anticipating anything about the movement of the ball. Hence, one of the most important attributes of a good tennis player is that he possesses a memory bank filled with stored impressions of tennis experience—of balls going back and forth, body movements, forehands, backhands, serves, volleys, smashes and the like. Tennis is learned as the nervous system coordinates the visual images of the ball's comings and goings with the feelings of the body's responses. The memory of a particular ball's approach is assimilated along with the memory of the body's movements in response, which in turn is coordinated with the feedback from the results of the body's action: the memory of the ball leaving the racket and landing in the other court. A person who did not have these experiences logged in his memory could not be expected to play tennis.

But is this all that is needed? An extensive set of memories and perhaps a coordinated body in good condition? Would two players of equal physical attributes play equal tennis just because they had each hit ten thousand similar shots? No. A great deal depends on the *quality* of the memory bank. If one player, while hitting his ten thousand shots, is bored or anxious, his experiences will not be of the same quality as the player who hits his ten thousand shots with a mind that is calm and interested.

Imagine that you are taking a motion picture of a tennis match. You are holding the camera in your hands, and for some reason you are a bit nervous, so your hands are shaking. What is the experience going to look like recorded on film, the camera's memory? Obviously it will be blurred, making it difficult to see the action clearly. How clearly you can see any given part of the match will depend on how shaky your hands were at that instant. Conversely, if your hands were steady the developed film will give a clear picture, and because of the clarity of the film memory more will be learned.

But it is also possible to hit a lot of tennis balls with a calm mind and still not acquire a good memory bank, especially if you are bored. When the mind is in the state called boredom, we don't learn much from our experiences—indeed, we can barely recall them. It's like taking a motion picture of the tennis match with so many filters in front of the lens that not enough light comes through. As a result, when you look at the film there is not enough contrast to see well what happened; the images are just an undifferentiated gray, with a few traces of movement. When nothing is vivid, not much is learned. In short, in order to record experiences in such a way that we can learn from them the mind should be not only still, but also interested.

Calmness and interest are two of the qualities of mind which make it so easy for a child to learn. He also has one other important attribute: his mind is uncluttered, open and free of concepts which distort perceptions. The adult mind, which is filled with concepts about how things are and should be, has difficulty experiencing anything but how it *thinks* things are. To use the film analogy again, this is a little like double exposure on a film. It's best to record new experiences on unused film—that is, to let go of what you think you know and to pay attention only to what is happening in front of you.

In sum, the qualities of the memory bank of a good tennis player are (1) *quantity* (he will have a lot of memories of a great variety of tennis experience—serves, spins, styles of play, and so forth—logged in his memory); (2) *clarity* (he will be able to focus on his memories later because the mind which the experience passed through was calm); (3) *intensity* (the images in his memory will be vivid because the mind was interested); (4) *an uncluttered mind* (the images will be undistorted because they are relatively free of concepts).

Thus, the state of mind which allows for the greatest awareness is that which maximizes both learning and performance at any level of play. The mind is in such a state when it is calm, clear and concentrated. In advanced tennis the ball is traveling so fast that a moment's mental distraction can throw off your timing. Also, tightening only one or two extra muscles at the wrong time can throw the ball off course enough to make you lose the point. To be aware enough to know when you are beginning to get out of the groove is essential to the advanced player of any sport. At any level of proficiency, a player can always further increase awareness of himself and of what is happening around him. As he increases his awareness, his performance automatically improves; he sees more, and therefore responds more appropriately to the situation. Fears, mistrust of oneself, trying hard and lapses in concentration all interfere with awareness—and therefore with learning and performance. I believe that the great advances in athletic performance will come primarily not because of increased physical conditioning or better techniques, but because of advances in our abilities to concentrate our minds and free ourselves from mental limitations.

Experience Is the Teacher

The Inner Game approach is to regard experience itself as the primary teacher. You can learn everything you need to know through awareness only of your own experience. In this approach the role of teachers is simply to help provide learning situations and to facilitate the progress of learning from experience. Teachers who can help you to increase your awareness of the significant part of an experience and guide you to new experiences are performing a valuable service which will help you in every part of your life. They become much more important to you than technicians or sources of information. But if they *distract* you from experience, imposing concepts which you then substitute for experience itself, you will benefit much less.

The Principle of Nonjudgment

Perhaps the most important step a person can take to increase awareness of the events in his experience, whether on a tennis court or off, is to try to rid himself of the concepts of "good" and "bad." My own experience with the Inner Game has shown me over and over that this is an essential step. As long as we look at our shots as either good or bad, we lose awareness of important details and inevitably become enmeshed in the Self 1 process of trying too hard. When we see a "bad" shot we will try hard to do better; when we see a "good" one we will try hard to do it again. When we see ourselves as bad, we attempt to improve and consequently lose all touch with natural growing. Because we don't like to look at what's "bad," we tend to ignore such an experience. But if you hit a ball three feet beyond the base line, it is not important to label the ball as bad; what *is* important is to see exactly where it lands so that you can learn from it. If you have ever watched people bowl, you will notice how often a bowler, seeing that his shot is not going to be a strike, will turn away so that he doesn't have to see where his ball *did* hit. Because of his judgment of the event as bad, he deprives himself of information that his body needs to make an accurate correction. Think how long it would take to hit a target with a rifle if you never looked at where your shots hit.

Judging one's self is even more devastating to growth and learning than judging one's performance. The player who decides that he isn't any good will soon be playing that way. One who decides that he's in a slump will stay there until he decides that he has pulled out of it. One of Self 1's favorite pastimes is to judge itself and others. It loves to measure how good and bad it is relative to others or to some hypothetical standards. Such self-judgment distorts perception, interferes with performance and retards our potential to learn.

A novice tennis player is not *bad* any more than a baby is *bad*. There are no "bad" tennis players; there are only players at different levels of physical and mental development. A flower is not *better* when it blooms than when it is merely a bud; at each stage it is the same thing, a flower in the process of expressing its potential. When we manage to let go of the notions of good people and bad people, a good me and a bad me, the process of our development is greatly facilitated. When tennis players learn to stop judging every shot, they become more willing to trust themselves and to swing more freely and accurately. When they stop being overcautious and overcontrolled, they become more open to experience and to learning real discrimination.

But for most people the process of letting go of judgments is a gradual one, and one which needs some practical methods to encourage it. This principle of nonjudgmental awareness is the basis of the Inner Game approach to learning and performance. Therefore the remainder of this book will elaborate on this principle and offer some practical methods for decreasing the obstacles to increased awareness and to the expression of our potential. At the end we will examine one important balancing ingredient: the will to win. To make it easier to go from A to B, the Inner Game approach suggests (1) increasing your awareness of A (where you are now); (2) increasing your awareness of B (what you wish to achieve); and (3) increasing your will to overcome the obstacles between the two.

2
Leaving Your Mind and Coming to Your Senses

The Art of Seeing What Is

If learning and performance are heightened primarily by increasing one's awareness, then what does one increase awareness of in tennis? There are only three principal events that occur in the game: (1) the ball comes toward you; (2) your body responds with some action; (3) the ball leaves you. Of these three events, two are known primarily through our visual sense; thus, it could be said that two-thirds of tennis lies in seeing the ball. There is also a court and a net to be aware of, but these are stable. The movement of your opponent or doubles partner is also important, but it is not fundamental to your hitting the ball well.

For those who are not reading this chapter mainly for the sake of improving their tennis, the flight of the ball can be taken as a metaphor. In any human activity, events seem to come toward us, we respond, and then the events leave us, bearing the mark of our response. I see the dartboard; I throw the dart; I see where it lands. I see and hear a person talking to me; I respond; I watch and listen to the answer. I see a problem; I take an action; I observe the results of my action. The clarity with which we see the oncoming event (in tennis the ball coming toward us) is crucial to the way we respond to it. Likewise, our perception of the departing event

—that is, the result of our action—has great influence on the way we will respond to similar events in the future. Seeing well is crucial to doing well at anything.

In spite of how often tennis players repeat to themselves the time-honored dictum "Look at the ball" the moments when a tennis ball is actually seen for what it is are remarkably rare. It is one thing to *look at* a ball and another thing to *see* it. Usually when we look at a ball approaching us, we see our thoughts projected onto it instead of the ball itself. In short, we see a high forehand coming, or a tricky slice, or a shot "I'm probably going to hit long again," or one "I probably won't reach."

But a ball is simply a ball, a furry sphere moving at a certain speed and direction. That's all. Neither backhands nor forehands, neither hard shots nor easy ones fly over the net—just balls. To really see well the speed and direction of an oncoming ball, we must subtract the concepts we project onto it; only then can we see and respond to each ball as it really is. When we accomplish this, Self 2's computer will receive the data it needs to send accurate instructions to the muscles which move us toward the ball and control the stroke. If we can understand the relationship between the way we see a tennis ball and the way we end up hitting it, we will automatically learn something about how our actions in general are influenced by our way of seeing.

The "Uh-oh" Experience

Perhaps the most common example of distorted seeing on or off the tennis courts is what I have come to call the "uh-oh experience." I discovered this phrase one day while watching two advanced players engaged in a long rally. On about the tenth shot, Paul hit a ball deep to John's backhand corner and rushed to the net. John, who had always considered deep backhands his greatest weakness, seemed to lose his composure. His lips tightened and his neck jutted forward while his feet shuffled backward hurriedly. Jerking his racket back at the last possible second, he flailed away, and as he saw his shot land just wide of the alley, he exclaimed, "There I go again!"

"What was the last thought you remember before hitting that shot?" I asked later.

"Just 'uh-oh, here comes another deep backhand!' " said John ruefully.

I realized that John's error had originated in his mind even before he had moved his racket. It was not a lack of sufficient talent or technique but his actual perception of the ball which had lost him the point. He had not really seen the ball; rather, he was watching all his past backhand errors approaching him. A threat was coming toward his weakness, so he tightened and retreated. Half of him wanted to defend himself; the other half wanted to strike out against his aggressor. Like Don Quixote, he defended himself against an illusionary monster and struck out.

If John's mind had been content to see only the ball coming toward him, without the "uh-oh," he undoubtedly could have returned it. It was the "uh-oh" in the mind that was responsible for the tightness in his arm, causing the racket to jerk and the ball to be mis-hit. The ball seen through an "uh-oh" usually appears to be approaching just a little faster and deeper than it actually is. Without the "uh-oh" it's merely a ball with a certain speed and direction. In fact, if John had not insisted on identifying the required stroke as a backhand, he might have been free to hit it with his forehand!

John's problem is a universal one in human perception. In an infinitesimal split second the mind tends to interpret—on the basis of impressions of similar events in the past—what the eye sees as some kind of personal threat. If the mind sees something coming toward its weakness, it thinks, in effect, "Uh-oh, here comes my mistake again," and inevitably there is an involuntary tightening of muscles which interferes with the natural and appropriate responses. This tightening of unnecessary muscles is undoubtedly the primary physical cause of errors in tennis and other sports, and it originates solely in the player's mind.

If you watch a relatively inexperienced player, you will see the "uh-oh" written across his face as almost every ball approaches. Eyebrows rise in apprehension and cheeks tighten. Tightness is also visible in shoulders, arms and legs, causing a characteristic jerk of the racket and staccato footwork. When volleying at net one can often see a player's ambivalence expressed by the racket lurching out toward the ball while the near foot retreats in the opposite direction. Even top-flight players are affected by the "uh-ohs" when faced with a shot that challenges their competence, such as when looking down the barrel of an overhead smash. Just as with a beginner, a few extra muscles tighten and the racket jerks toward the ball too abruptly. Such a moment demands a precision which emanates only from a calm mind and a smooth, quick movement. The racket must move before a thought can interrupt its accuracy. When the player is able to move quicker than his thought, without the interruption of an "uh-oh," you see the spectacular return that seems impossible to everyone—especially to the hitter himself.

The "uh-ohs" seem to become loudest when we are most doubting our competence. The response is triggered by self-doubt, and is magnified in those situations which we think matter the most. If I doubt my serve, I may experience some tightness during the first game, but I'm apt to experience a lot more during the last. I will hear a louder "uh-oh" on a crucial point in an "important" match with people watching than I will while practicing with a bucket of balls on a deserted court at dusk. But it is just when we think that the point really *does* matter that we want to be able to play without the "uh-ohs." It is *then* that we need quickness and accuracy without overtightness.

An embarrassing example of how much better we sometimes play when it doesn't count often presents itself on the return of serve. How many times have you seen a blistering serve speeding toward you, even to your weakness, but seeing that it will land a few inches long, you yell "Fault!" and knock it back for what would have been an indisputable winner? Dammit, why can't I do that when the serve is in? you wonder as you remember your weak, tentative return, which is usually put away by your opponent. And of course the return that didn't count has landed much closer to the line than you would have ever dared aim for. Perfect flow and perfect timing! It's frustrating and embarrassing, but that's how well Self 2 can hit the ball when Self 1 isn't feeling threatened, isn't tightening, isn't trying. It's a good idea to pay attention to this experience whenever it happens because it gives you concrete evidence of the superior ability of Self 2. It establishes a basis for the requisite trust in Self 2, so that someday you can learn to rely on it even when it counts.

The "uh-oh" experience is not always triggered by something coming *at* you. Often it occurs because of the way we perceive a static situation. For example, in golf I tend to believe that I can't hit short chip shots well. Often my wrist wobbles just before the club meets the ball and an easy shot is turned into a disaster. Therefore, when I see that I am a few yards off the green on the fringe, I tend to think, Uh-oh, here comes another duff. There is a quick image in my mind of that wobble, and I start thinking about how to make sure it doesn't happen this time. My practice stroke—when it doesn't count—is flawless; firm and sure, I address the ball, view the flag and take a firm, sure swing. But when addressing the ball for the actual shot, I tighten my hands a little more to make sure that I'm holding the club firmly. Then it happens; somewhere between my downswing and the moment of actual contact, that old wobble jumps out from nowhere and destroys my shot, my score and my self-confidence!

Once my father told me about a golfer who became exasperated with his game while playing a round with Sam Snead. On the 12th hole he finally turned to Sam for help. "What is it I'm doing wrong?" he asked. "Just one thing," answered Snead. "You don't hit the ball with your practice swing."

We tend to choke in those situations in which we remember choking before. First we think, I'll probably choke in this situation, then proceed to do so. A player may have been serving well, but when the score reaches 30–40, 4–5, the thought occurs to him, Uh-oh, I might double-fault and lose the set. The memories of past double faults on a crucial point enter the mind, and the past is projected onto the present. Entertaining these memories, the player is on his way to a double fault even before he lifts his racket.

Ball-Tossing Demonstration. To observe how our seeing affects our response, try this simple demonstration. Pick a person who considers himself a little uncoordinated, someone who is not sure of himself in catching balls, and from a few feet away toss him a tennis ball. Watch his reactions. Usually the head will jerk backwards a bit, the eyebrows will jump up, and the hands, opened wider than necessary, will dart uncertainly toward the ball. After several tosses, change your instruction; this time ask the person simply to watch the seams of the ball and see if he can count the number of times the ball revolves while it approaches. Then watch his response. Usually there will be fewer, if any, signs of alarm on his face, and his hands will move much more economically and smoothly, with fewer misses. When trying to *catch* a ball, a person doesn't see it well, but when trying to *see* it, he catches very well.

The Perception, Response, Self-Image Cycle

The above experiment demonstrates the interesting relationship between perception, response and self-image. If my image of myself is that I can't catch balls well (or hit them with a tennis racket), when one comes toward me I *perceive* it as a threat. My response is to tighten, causing me to move awkwardly and inaccurately. When I perceive my awkwardness and its results—a dropped ball, or one hit out of the court—I am confirmed in my negative self-image, and my belief in my inability is strengthened. This means that the next time I see a ball coming toward me, I will again misperceive it. The misperception of the ball leads directly to a distortion in my response, and the distortion in my response leads me to a distorted self-image, which in turn affects the way I perceive the next ball. This basic vicious circle operates in tennis players at all levels of competence, and unless the circle is broken, the player will improve only very slowly, if at all.

This chapter and the next one are about how to break out of this circle perceptually—that is, by altering our "seeing."

Before introducing the first exercise in seeing, I want to give an example of the "uh-oh" experience off the court. The one that comes most readily to mind is how often parents misperceive the behavior of their children. If I am working on a chapter of this book while my six-year-old boy is playing loudly in the next room, I am likely to perceive an annoyance. Hearing the noise as a threat to my concentration, I think "Uh-oh, here comes another disturbance," my mind and body tighten, and my ears try to close. Then I am filled with thoughts about how to put an end to the noise. My son may be shouting with glee or in frustration; he may be an Apache on the warpath or just quarreling with his sister; it doesn't really matter to the listener. But in focusing on how to stop the noise, I miss the important details of the event and do not have sufficient awareness to respond appropriately. I may or may not rid myself of this distraction for the moment, but the chances are I won't do much either for my relationship with Richard or for his growing sense of responsibility. If, on the other hand, I choose either to tune out the noise or to listen to it for what it really is, my response will be more appropriate. I will have one response for the wild Indian, and quite another for the quarrel with Lynn. The key to the best response lies in the details of the commotion. If the "uh-oh" deafens me to what is really happening, I'm apt to start overswinging at something I have misperceived.

Overcoming the "Uh-ohs"

The fundamental principle behind techniques for ridding oneself of the "uh-ohs" is to focus your mind on something actual. The "uh-oh" happens when the mind is focused on itself—that is, when the mind allows its own thought to be projected onto the actual event. As the mind is allowed to become more interested in the *actual* details of an event, it forgets its fear and the volume of the "uh-oh" decreases.

"Bounce-Hit"

Molly, who was about forty-five, five feet tall and weighed close to 160 pounds, had never held a tennis racket in her hand before. She played no sports at all and spent her leisure hours playing bridge; she was good enough at it to have attained the level of Life Master. But tennis was another matter and she was very doubtful about her ability to learn the sport. She came to the court only because she had been asked to by a friend of mine, who told her that I needed

someone who had never played tennis in order to demonstrate a new technique of teaching for a television news program.

Wearing an old pair of tennis shoes and a muumuu which
came to her ankles, Molly took one look at the cameras and
said, "Uh-oh, I knew I shouldn't have come. Why do I need
to make a fool of myself for the whole world to see?"

All I could think to say to reassure her was, "Molly, I
promise not to ask you to do anything that you won't be able
to do. Please give it a try." She looked at me skeptically, but
assented.

When it came time for the demonstration, I gave Molly the
following instruction: "All I want you to do is to watch the
tennis ball and say 'Bounce' when the ball hits the court, and
'Hit' when it hits my racket."

I tapped the ball into the air a few times, letting it bounce
so that she could practice. Finding this simple, Molly looked
relieved, and I asked her to continue the awareness drill at
the base line of the court while I hit a few balls thrown to
me by someone standing in front of the net. "Just say
'Bounce' the instant the ball hits the court coming toward
me, 'Hit' as it meets the strings of my racket, and then
'Bounce' again when it lands on the other side of the net."

I hit about ten or twelve forehands and backhands, listening closely to Molly's voice as I did so for signs of tension
and to hear how closely her voice corresponded to the actual
bounce and hit of the ball. Soon her "Bounces" and "Hits"
were even and accurate and she seemed to have forgotten her
fear of the cameras.

"Now I want you to stand just where I was standing," I
told her. "When I throw the ball to you, I want you to
continue to say "Bounce" when it bounces, and say 'Hit'
when you *would* hit it. But don't hit it; just let it go by."

I threw Molly five balls and noticed that her voice was
considerably higher-pitched and more strained on the "Hit"
than on the "Bounce." But after about ten balls thrown to
each side of her, her voice again seemed relaxed and even.
"Now, whenever you feel like it, let your racket swing and
say 'Hit' when the ball meets the strings," I said.

Molly let a few go by, then hit the first ball of her life over
the net with astonishing gracefulness. "Wow!" she said in
astonishment. "That's fun." She hit the next three, but none

went over. With each ball she said "Bounce" before it bounced and "Hit" considerably after contact. Her voice was loud, almost angry on the "Hit," and on the last shot she didn't even say the word.

"Are your 'Bounces' and 'Hits' on those first four balls on time, early or late?" I asked, expressing interest only in the awareness drill and not in the results of her strokes.

"Oh, I don't really know. After the first shot, I was just trying to hit the ball over."

"You don't need to worry about hitting the ball over for a while. Let's get back to simply seeing the ball. I want to find out whether your 'Bounces' and 'Hits' are in synch with the ball, and if you can tell whether they are early or late."

Three more balls.

"I'm a little early on the 'Bounce,' and a little late on the 'Hit,' " Molly reported with interest. Three more balls. "Now they're pretty much on time."

After the next two minutes Molly was hitting most of her shots over the net with a swing in which her body faced the net. Then her feet began moving, first sideways with the right, then stepping forward with the left. Soon she experimented by stepping in with her right foot. After only a minute of this, she began moving her right foot slightly to the side. After a few minutes more, she was stepping consistently sideways with her right foot and stepping diagonally across the body with her left, close to textbook perfection. Her face looked at ease, interested and curious.

"What's happening with your feet?" I asked.

"I don't know. They seem to be moving a little more than when I began."

"Are you moving them on purpose?" I asked, mainly for the sake of the cameras.

"No. I'm just doing 'bounce-hit,' and not thinking about anything. This is really fun."

The rest of the process was quite simple. After a few minutes I was throwing Molly running forehands and backhands. (She had unconsciously changed her grip on the backhand after about the tenth shot!) After no more than fifteen minutes, we were rallying with each other across the net. "Bounce—Hit . . . bounce—hit . . . bounce—hit," Molly called out whenever the ball hit our rackets or bounced on either side of the court. Some of our rallies lasted ten or twelve shots. "I'm really getting into the rhythm," she said, expressing little excitement but a lot of interest. I could tell that her mind was absorbed and not easily distracted either by her occasional complete misses or by some of the remarkable shots she hit on the run.

I used another awareness exercise to help Molly learn the serve, and after only five minutes of practice she served an entire game against me without a double fault. On the average, the points lasted four or five shots, and by the end of the game only twenty-five minutes had elapsed since the lesson began—the time allotted by the program to demonstrate how much one student could learn from scratch without receiving any technical instructions.

Afterwards Molly was most surprised by how she had been able to move. "I ran after balls in a way I never thought I'd be able to. I didn't think about it, but I did it." Other than that, she was not much surprised at how fast she had learned to play because she didn't have anything to compare it to. "I almost didn't come today," she said, "because I thought tennis was a lot harder to learn than it really is."

"I see," said Bob, the producer of the show, himself an avid tennis player, "the bounce-hit exercise is primarily a device for keeping the mind calm so that the body can hit the ball. 'Bounce-hit' is kind of like a mantra, isn't it?"

"Well, the rhythmic verbalizing does have a calming effect on the nervous system, but it's more than that. It focuses the attention on something actual—the ball. Seeing the ball coming toward it and seeing the results—its departure—Molly's computer automatically began to make adjustments and refinements in the instructions it gave her muscles. These instructions are nonverbal, and are too sophisticated to put into words."

"But what was the point of having Molly say 'Bounce—hit' while *you* were hitting the ball at the beginning of the exercise?" asked Bob. "I noticed that you didn't ask her to pay any attention to your stroke."

"The first point was to give Molly's Self 2 some input about how a tennis ball behaves on a tennis court, without the distractions that tend to intrude once she also has to hit the ball. Very few beginners are given this opportunity. Secondly, when Molly said 'Hit,' she was watching so carefully that she couldn't *help* but see my stroke when the ball hit my racket. At that instant her Self 2 was picking up information about the elements of the forehand and backhand. Without consciously thinking about it, she saw that you didn't have to swing hard or do anything fancy to produce the desired results. If I had told her to pay close attention to my stroke, she would probably have been saying to herself, 'Oh, you're supposed to step sideways with your right foot and forward with your left foot . . . Your racket is supposed to go back low and end up high,' and so forth. Then she would have tried to imitate me, and become as frustrated as if I had given her all those instructions verbally. She certainly wouldn't have been as spontaneous and natural as she was after twenty minutes."

The bounce-hit drill is a deceptively simple exercise; indeed, to more advanced players, it often seems too simple to be very effective. The difficulty in doing it well lies in the inability to focus only on bounce-hit. Most players find it simple to say "Bounce" and "Hit" on time and still entertain a number of thoughts about *how* to hit the ball. They will say "Bounce—hit," and then still *try* to hit it. What must be practiced for best results is to let go of trying to hit the ball right, and to concentrate the mind totally on the ball, listening to the changes in cadence. It is not unusual for two players to double or triple the length of their rallies when performing this awareness exercise.

Watching intermediate and advanced players do this exercise is revealing. Each tends to be able to stay focused on the "bounce-hit" only as long as the shot seems to them easy at their level of competence (or imagined competence). But as soon as they see a tough one coming, the "Bounce" tends to get said a fraction of a second beforehand (anxious anticipation), and the "Hit" often isn't said until the ball is on its way toward the net. As soon as we see a *difficulty* approaching instead of a ball, it is hard not to become involved in trying to hit it, instead of putting our attention on the *seeing* of it. When we actually perceive it as it is, the body has a chance to hit it according to the best of its ability. So if you are an intermediate or advanced player practicing this drill, from time to time you should make yourself aware of just how much of your conscious attention is really on the exercise and how much on trying to hit the ball. If you simply notice the difference in these two states and observe the results both while hitting when you are trying and hitting while you are not, you will automatically approach the state of mind which works best for you.

There is a further refinement of bounce-hit which encourages intermediate or advanced players to let go a little more of their "uh-ohs." This involves attending to further detail. Instead of simply watching the ball bounce and hit, the player who needs to absorb more of his attention on the ball can also *listen* to the ball bouncing on the court and then hitting the racket. Then he can compare the timing of the sound of his own voice with that of the ball. Doing this drill with precision is almost guaranteed to so absorb the mind that it cannot bother Self 2 while it hits the ball.

Once, during an Inner Game clinic, four people at different times told me they noticed that their voice was much louder and more aggressive on the "Hit" than on the "Bounce," and each wondered if it would help if he used a word other than "hit." It was an interesting observation. If you take the word "hit" as a command instead of an observation of the instant that the ball meets the racket, you are apt to be a little overstrained both in your tone of voice and in your body movement. Listening to the tone of your voice when performing this exercise is a revealing way to get in touch with how much you are trying. Often it is easier to hear the tension in your voice than to feel it in your body. Of course, there is nothing sacred in the words "bounce-hit"; the same effect could be achieved by saying "One, two." Do whatever works for you. (Note: Naturally it is not always convenient or appropriate to say "Bounce—hit" out loud, but at least let your lips mouth the words; otherwise, you are likely to get out of synch with the ball.)

Ball Rising or Falling at Contact

Although the bounce-hit exercise has proven effective in inducing concentration and has now become quite well known, there are similar exercises which can be just as effective. One such which more advanced players have appreciated is to attempt to discern whether the ball is still rising, is level, or is falling at the instant that it makes contact with your racket and that of your opponent. The principle is the same. Self 1 becomes calm as it concentrates on factual detail, and gets out of the way of Self 2, which then hits the ball unimpeded, according to its ability.

I never tire of seeing the kind of natural learning process which takes place when the mind is calm. It is beautiful to watch, and it all works because of a little trick (even if the trick is exposed, it still works): give the ever-thinking mind something subtle and exact enough to hold its attention, and the body will be left free to perform according to its natural endowments.

This kind of freedom almost never happens all at once, and even when it does, you can certainly expect Self 1 to return and try to regain some of its lost sense of control. Though you may experience dramatically superior performance when Self 2 is in charge, amazingly enough there is still that other part of us which wants to take over, and until we become more confident in Self 2 we will tend to let Self 1 be dominant. The process is gradual. As you increase awareness of the difference between *seeing* and *trying,* you will naturally let Self 1 shed more and more of its control.

Some players pick up an Inner Game drill as a gimmick, to see if it "works," try it once or twice without improvement, and decide that it isn't for them. But the awareness exercises in the Inner Game are not gimmicks; if you perform them in the right spirit, they will definitely help your concentration—and concentration always "works."

"Bounce-Hit" off the Court

The principle behind "bounce-hit" applies to any situation. The idea is to learn to separate your mind's reaction to an event from the event itself. It is the practice of detached seeing, and its basic requirement is acceptance of the situation as it is without wishing it to be different. Only then can you see events clearly enough to be able to respond appropriately.

One of the best examples of the "bounce-hit" principle off the court was given by the astronauts in their dealing with various emergencies in space. No matter how critical the situation seemed, they kept their minds focused on the relevant spacecraft indicators while reporting back to their control center in Houston. Concentrating on concrete details allowed their minds to remain calm even in critical situations —perhaps even more critical than match point—and to take appropriate action moment by moment.

When the astronauts found it necessary they asked Houston Control Center for direction. It could be said that every human being has a Houston control center, with an enormous computer capable of storing and collating an immense amount of detailed information, and then of issuing precise instructions. We all have a Self 2, but somehow, like Hal, the computer in *2001: A Space Odyssey,* we have taken on a separate identity—Self 1—which always wants to take control, and which, seeing through the eyes of its distorted self, takes distorted actions.

The Art of Seeing the Results of One's Actions

So far we have been talking about getting rid of the anxiety which distorts our perception of an approaching event, especially of a tennis ball coming toward us. However, the mind also distorts the departing event, the ball leaving the racket, which is the result of our action, but in a different way. We tend to look on the results with a *judging* eye, seeing our shots in terms of "good" or "bad." Usually we don't judge the approaching event because we don't assume personal responsibility for it.

The first problem with becoming involved in judging our actions is that it makes it extremely hard to really perceive what has happened. Players seldom *see* where balls that go out of court really land; they simply don't like to notice the details of shots they label as "bad." Consequently Self 2 does not get the accurate feedback it needs to make corrections in its stroke. But it needs to know exactly where each ball has landed in order to learn from the event. What it *doesn't* really need to know is that the shot was "bad," or that it is "a clumsy fool" for missing a shot.

Seeing your shots land in and out accurately and with

detachment is not easy. Look at the faces of players and you will see how habituated most are to judging every shot they make. Unfortunately, the judgment, whether good or bad, always seems to lead to trying harder the next time. "Bad" shots we analyze and try to correct; "good" shots we analyze and try to reproduce. In each case the analysis and the trying get in the way of our own excellence.

Errors: A Part of Learning

Any kind of learning requires accurate feedback on the results of our actions, and in order to get such feedback it is essential that we let go of our fear of making errors. The contemporary idea in learning theory that trial and error is an outmoded way of learning, because errors give the student a sense of failure, is nonsense, in my opinion. Trial and error is the way we learn, like it or not. What we need to eliminate is not occasional mistakes, but our *fear* of mistakes and the sense of failure we attach to them. When players get over this fear of mistakes, they stop making so many. Self 2 can learn just as much from an error as from a winner, so in terms of the future an error can be as valuable as a winner by helping the body to discriminate between the effective and the ineffective.

The importance of increasing a student's awareness of results made a strong impression on me one day when I was giving a lesson to a former baseball player turned movie producer. Ted, who had just taken up the game, loved hitting the ball hard but seldom hit one in the court. Most of his forehands landed at least six feet long, and three out of ten hit the fence on the fly. What amazed me was that this didn't seem to bother him. He wanted to be a great player right away, and so long as each shot had power he seemed quite content to hit a bomb every time. I knew that if I started lecturing Ted about what he was doing wrong and the necessity of keeping the ball in court, he might become overcautious and lose the asset of his free swing.

"Mark the Spot"

"Ted, let's play a game called 'mark the spot,'" I suggested. "Whenever I ask you, I want you to show me the exact spot on the court where the last ball bounced." Ted agreed, and during the next five minutes I asked him a dozen times to point to the place on the court where *my* last ball had landed. At first Ted was accurate within two feet, but after a few minutes he was usually within six inches. Then I started asking him to tell me where *his* shots were landing. At first he would say "Out" or "Long" with seeming indifference.

"How far?" I would ask.

On balls that landed twelve feet out he would reply, "Oh, I don't know—about three or four feet, I guess."

I was amazed at how much less accurate Ted's perception was of the ball leaving him than of one approaching him, and when I pointed this out to him, he became curious. Now he was ready to be introduced to "depth perception," an awareness game designed to increase further one's perception of results.

Depth Perception. "In this exercise, after you see each of your shots bounce, call out the number of feet you estimate that the ball landed from the base line, either long or short. If it lands three feet short, just say 'Three'; if it lands two feet long, say 'Plus two.' If it lands on the line, that's a 'Zero.' To make your estimates easier, since the distance from the base line to the service line is eighteen feet, a ball that bounces midway between the lines would be a 'nine.' Now, the point of this drill is not to try to see how close you can come to hitting the base line. All we're trying to do is to see how accurately you can observe exactly where your ball lands. This is simply an awareness drill to increase your depth perception."

"I understand," said Ted, and we began.

"Plus five. Plus eight. Plus two. Zero. Plus six. Plus five." Ted's balls were zooming across, but his perception was still way off, often by six or more feet; what he called "zero" had landed four feet long. Every so often I would tap my racket on the spot where the ball had actually landed and call out the number of feet. It sounded like this:

Ted: Plus five. Plus three. Plus six.

Tim: Plus twelve.

Ted: Really? Plus six. Plus eight. Plus four.

Tim: Plus nine.

Ted: Really? Plus ten. Plus eight. Plus—oh, I guess, fourteen.

Tim: Plus fourteen! Right. You saw it! Now continue hitting out as long as you like, but keep observing where the balls bounce.

It took about five minutes before Ted stopped distorting and allowed himself to really *see* where his balls were landing. I expressed no concern about how far out any shot was; I was interested only in the accuracy of his observations. But what surprised me was that even though his perceptions had become more accurate, the consistency in his shots that I had expected would automatically result simply didn't appear. Ted was still spraying balls all over the place, though now he called out the lengths with accuracy. He seemed to be playing the game, but apparently it wasn't improving his tennis.

I must admit that at this point I felt like trying to correct Ted's stroke, which was very erratic. He had four different swings which he seemed to employ at random, and most of them imparted underspin or sidespin to the ball. But I resisted the temptation, risking my credibility in Ted's eyes. This increase in awareness has to work eventually, I felt. Ted's brain had been getting the feedback it needed for five minutes, and I assumed he wished to improve, so I was determined to continue and see what happened. Besides, I was getting curious as to how long it would take.

Ted hit the next ten balls in his usual random way, but then at last it began to happen: he hit three shots in a row with topspin, each of them landing about four feet inside the base line.

"Four . . . three . . . four . . . one . . . plus two . . . four . . . six . . ." Ted was calling out, quite unaware that one of his four strokes, the one that produced topspin and brought the ball down into the court, was now becoming dominant. We continued for ten more minutes, and he hit at least 80 percent of his shots within the base line. For the first time, he had the necessary control.

Ted was ecstatic. "So this is what tennis is!" he exclaimed. "I don't really know how I'm doing it, but that's okay. I really like it."

I still didn't really understand why the change had taken so long, but I had a guess. Often a student will test his Inner Game teacher and his Self 2. In effect the teacher is saying, "Hit the ball wherever you like, but watch where it goes." Self 1 smells a trick and says to itself, "This is just a gimmick to get me to improve. He's really going to be judging me to see how well I do." Something in the student needs to test the teacher's acceptance level, but when he discovers that the teacher isn't threatened by poor performance, his own self-judgment relaxes, allowing him to see and experiment. When judgment is erased, the conditions for natural learning are met and change occurs simply because there is nothing to resist it.

Depth perception is also an extremely effective awareness game for advanced players. Any player's skill develops naturally as he becomes more observant of the results of his shots. But the advanced player must discriminate by inches rather than feet. A little practice in accurate discrimination of this kind is extremely effective.

(Note: A nice extension of this drill is to call out to yourself as soon as you can where you anticipate your opponent's ball will land after it leaves his racket. This increases your ability to perceive the approaching ball, and therefore heightens the accuracy of your anticipation. If calling out the number of feet from the base line the ball will land seems too confusing, then divide the court into, say, four sections and simply judge where it will bounce—1, 2, 3 or 4.)

"Height"

The same approach can be used to gain greater control of the height at which the ball is hit over the net. In the awareness exercise I call "height," the player calls out the number of feet each ball passes over or below the net cord. It's surprising how quickly this can produce consistency in elevation. Once again, as Self 2's brain gets better feedback, its instructions to the muscles become more refined. After all, there are only two main requirements to the game: to hit the ball over the net and into the court, and if you did this every time you would win Wimbledon. Therefore, it makes sense to develop your ability to perceive height, depth and width. It's really quite simple: you learn complicated stroke technique simply by increasing your awareness of the results of your actions. If you learn how to see, Self 2 will take care of learning how to hit.

Topspin and Underspin on the Ski Slope

One day I decided to go skiing for the first time in ten years. After experimenting a bit with the Inner Game of skiing, I found myself riding on the lift with one of the instructors. Naturally, I asked him some leading questions, and he gave me an elaborate dissertation on correct form. I looked a bit overwhelmed and remarked that it sounded pretty complicated. Knowing that I was a tennis pro, he said, "Well, learning how to hit a topspin forehand is pretty complicated too, and skiing is no easier."

"Okay," I said, "let me teach you how to hit a topspin forehand, and in exchange you teach me how to ski by the same method."

He agreed, and we began. "If you wanted to learn how to hit a tennis ball with topspin, here's how I would help you," I said. "First, I would make sure you understood what topspin was." Holding an imaginary ball, I showed him how it spun in the same direction as its flight. "That's topspin. When it spins the opposite way, it's called 'underspin.' When there's no spin, you are hitting the ball flat. Then I would hit some balls to you, not to let you see how I did it, but to just ask you to differentiate between topspin and underspin. When you could detect the difference in spins, I would then ask you to start hitting balls yourself. As you increased your awareness of the kind of spin on each shot, your body would be educating itself, learning which stroke produced which result."

"But what if I got stuck hitting underspin and wanted to learn topspin?" asked Tom.

"Then you would start discriminating between different amounts of underspin. Instead of thinking that underspin was bad and had to be changed, you would begin to perceive that one shot had slightly less underspin than the last. Soon your body would be learning how to hit flat, and in a little while one ball would inevitably be hit with slight topspin. Whatever the body did to produce this topspin would be a newly learned movement, programmed into the body, which would soon learn how to increase the amount of topspin. In the long run you would be able to produce at will either kind of spin in varying degrees. Your body is really pretty smart if you are willing to trust it."

By now we had reached the top of the mountain, and I could tell that this instructor was going to tell me to trust my body and let it teach me how to ski down it.

Sure enough. "The aim of skiing is simple," my new friend said. "It is to learn to stay *on balance* while negotiating any kind of terrain."

In one sentence he had given me what I needed. Paying attention to balance would give me the feedback I needed most. I forgot about technique, concentrated only on balance, fell a few times and had the best run of my life. I was able to perceive when I began to lose balance, and what happened when my weight was over different skis. As a result I was much more aware of everything that happened, and the enjoyment of this particular run lodged itself in my memory so vividly that it brought me back to the slopes over and over.

Seeing the Results off the Court

Let's return to the example of my son who has been making a commotion in the next room. Maybe I walk in and say, "Richard, I'm having a difficult time concentrating on my writing because of all the noise in here." Or, "Richard, please be quiet; you shouldn't be roughhousing inside," or, "Richard, why don't you play outside for a while?" There are many alternative shots to make, and Richard has a lot of possible responses too. But all that is important to me is that I really see and hear his answer if I want to learn from the experience. If I don't watch and listen closely, I won't be able to tell the difference between hurt feelings and a con job, between natural resistance to change and disguised defiance.

What's more, Richard probably won't know the difference either.

Of course, what I learn will depend on my goals at that instant. If my mind is set simply on shutting Richard up, what I learn will depend on the resulting decibel levels. But if I am more interested in understanding and developing my relationship with Richard, I will need to pay attention to such details as my own tone of voice, words, gestures and so on. I also observe where my shot lands on Richard—that is, pay attention to his lower lip, body postures, and the tone of his response. It is from these that I will get feedback.

The messages sent between people are considerably more subtle than the spin on a tennis ball, and they are impossible to grasp unless we really want to see what's happening. This means being willing to let go of our judgments—likes and dislikes—of the events before us and ridding ourselves of our attachment to Self 1 to bring about certain results. Because of years of accepted programming, it takes practice to overcome our tendencies to judge and fix things up, but when we are willing to see and do, without the interference of Self 1, the rewards are strikingly apparent.

Summary

The way we see events approaching us affects the way we respond to them; the way we respond to them affects the way we regard ourselves; and this in turn affects the way we see new events. Our actions reflect the clarity of our perceptions. When we finally learn to let go of fear, we see and act at levels beyond what we imagined possible, and it is then that we begin to discover ourselves.

3
Overcoming Boredom

The "Ho-hum" Experience

There is another state of mind which distorts awareness and interferes with learning as much as the "uh-ohs": *boredom.* Whereas the "uh-oh" experience jiggles and warps our perception, boredom dulls perception and deadens our ability to respond to whatever we experience. Its effect is to drop a veil between awareness and our senses, allowing only the most obvious features of an experience to register on our consciousness and memory. Events seen through a bored mind seem lifeless and changeless, and as a result we lose our concentration. Boredom is a major enemy of natural learning.

Although most players realize that watching the ball is the most important task at all levels of play, relatively few of them actually *do* it. One moment we are watching the ball like a hawk; the next, our minds have wandered off and are thinking about something else entirely.

In my opinion the chief reason players have difficulty sustaining concentration is that they grow bored, primarily because of the frequency and repetitious nature of the ball's flight. All things common, ordinary, continual, frequent and obvious in time become barely noticed by the mind, which comes to assume that it knows all about them. So thinking, it loses its natural curiosity and attentiveness, and therefore its awareness. When we've seen 43,413 backhands coming toward us, it takes a special kind of awareness to see the 43,414th as a new event really worth paying attention to. Instead, we are apt to see it through the dense fog of a "ho-hum." This "ho-hum" so dulls our perception of the ball that we miss important details of its flight and therefore can't respond accurately to it, much less with our full energy. Also, our memory of the event is so colorless that afterwards we don't learn much from the experience. We both learn and perform at our peak levels only when the mind is alive, alert, curious, and enjoying itself. It's amazing how few educators really understand this basic aspect of learning.

"Ho-hum versus "Uh-oh"

The "ho-hum" experience presents an interesting contrast to the "uh-oh" one. Anxiety tends to decrease with repetition, while boredom increases, so it seems very likely that we use boredom as a kind of shield against "uh-ohs." The mind has an ability to hold on to concepts and expectations about the way things are, and soon almost everything looks just as we expected it to. We stop seeing what is new and different, and perceive only our own projected expectations. As a result there are few surprises, not much fun, and a sense of dullness called boredom that masks our anxiety. In this state we may be defended from the "uh-ohs," but we lose both our ability to appreciate common experiences and our alertness to detail.

Regaining this skill, one which we all possessed as small children before our minds were filled with limiting concepts, is important to the Inner Game player. He reasons that since by definition the commonplace is what is experienced most often, the talent to be able to appreciate it is extremely valuable. Therefore, this chapter addresses itself to the problem of how to increase one's level of interest and alertness in something as repetitious as a tennis ball. If we can enhance this skill, perhaps in the same way we can learn to appreciate the familiar and sometimes overfamiliar people, places and things that we often lose interest in—such as spouses, jobs, meals, air, trees, life, time and virtually everything else in our day-to-day existence.

Techniques for Seeing a Tennis Ball

The first thing to realize about taking one's eye off the ball is that prior to this act the mind has left. Don't blame your body. *The eyes are dependent on the interest of the mind.* The mind leaves the ball because it has become more interested in something else. You cannot expect to be able to concentrate on a tennis ball simply by telling yourself over and over, "Watch the ball, watch the ball, watch the ball." Sustaining attention, as in the "bounce-hit" exercise, requires *some* self-discipline, but it is primarily a matter of *allowing* yourself to become interested enough so that the mind *wants* to stay on the ball. When watching a good movie, we don't have to tell ourselves, "Watch the screen, watch the screen." This is the key to any practice of concentration: we learn and perform at our best only when we are genuinely interested—that is, when we have overcome both the "uh-oh" and the "ho-hum" in our minds.

"Seeing the Trajectory"

The key to finding interest in the commonplace lies first in forgetting limiting concepts and projections—for example, that a ball is simply something to return over the net—and secondly allowing the mind to be open to fresh detail. In preparation for an important match, Billie Jean King, a great student of concentration, used to gaze at a tennis ball in her hand and absorb the details of its seams, matted hair, shape, color and texture. She did this not because such details had any practical application, but because they aided her concentration, and she realized that anything which increases this state is helpful.

Yet even more interesting than the properties of a stationary ball are those of one *in motion.* Movement of any kind seems to interest the mind, and has ever since we were babies, even before we could recognize or identify objects. Tennis balls per se are hardly unique, but every ball hit by a racket carves a unique shape in space. Placing one's attention on the flow of this curved line made by a ball in flight has power to attract the mind's interest.

I call this exercise "seeing the trajectory." In performing it you ask your mind to focus not so much on the ball itself, but on its flight from racket to court to racket to court. You forget about seeing backhands or forehands, difficult shots or easy ones, or about how you're going to get into position. Instead you put your mind solely on the ball's path, letting the eye ride with the ball, experiencing whatever interests you during every foot of its flight. Some people may notice the different shapes of its curve—some flatter, some more parabolic. Others notice the exact point at which the ball stops rising, or the point at which it starts descending—whatever in the ball's trajectory catches their interest.

The person who allows his mind to grow absorbed in the ball's trajectory often finds himself playing beyond his normal levels; totally forgetting about footwork and strokes, he is usually surprised to find himself returning ball after ball effectively and effortlessly. But those who watch the trajectory yet also continue to think about the *how* of hitting the ball usually find their play less improved and their minds less absorbed. The art in "seeing the trajectory," as in all ball-awareness drills, is to completely lose oneself in the exercise and let the body respond spontaneously. When this occurs, there is not only an increase in the level of one's performance, but a heightened awareness of the act of playing tennis which is truly enjoyable. This enjoyment destroys any traces of boredom.

Still, some people have a hard time letting go of their accustomed way of seeing. For example, some players see each ball as a test of their competence, and as a result they alternate endlessly between anxiety and boredom. "Seeing the trajectory," done intently, has the power to replace achievement-oriented perception with a more aware kind of perception—one which ironically enhances achievement.

Having Fun

Sometimes if I am having difficulty breaking free of the frustration and boredom which comes from seeing every ball as a challenge or threat to my competence—an exhausting game that I've played since I was a kid—I decide to let go of all concern about how well I'm playing (or even how well I'm concentrating), and simply have fun. I stop trying to concentrate and begin to hit the ball the way I really want to, in whatever way will give me the most enjoyment, even if I miss it altogether. Sometimes I play better immediately, sometimes not, but it breaks the back of my boredom and therefore soon leads to better play and a fuller appreciation of the game.

The art of having fun in tennis is tragically lost by many players who become overly intent on the achievement aspects of the game. Fun may not be the *only* point in playing tennis, but if it is absent you are also missing the real point—and probably a lot of balls as well.

But the art in having fun does not lie in being undisciplined. Real fun happens whenever we become so involved in what we're doing that we lose ourselves in the activity. What do we lose? Self 1 and all its worries about our self-image, all its deadening concepts and expectations. Self 1 becomes so concentrated in the activity of the moment that we are free to experience without interference the natural enjoyment and excellence of Self 2.

Art Appreciation

One game which has helped many people to alter their usual way of seeing the ball is one called "art appreciation." This drill may sound far-fetched at first, but I wouldn't include it if it hadn't been so effective in achieving the higher levels of concentration necessary to "playing out of one's mind." The game is simple: you just look at the court and the net as a kind of three-dimensional canvas. Each new trajectory of the ball is then perceived as a new line on the drawing. The player sees the ball from an aesthetic point of view and regards its path as he would a line drawn by an artist. He notices not only the *shape* of the line, but the way it relates to others in the drawing, especially that of the net. To notice the relationship between the ball's trajectory and the net, and particularly to see the space between the two, demands great attention and therefore absorbs the mind. At the same time, this exercise forces sophisticated data about the clearance of the ball over the net and the exact margin of safety in respect to the lines to be absorbed by Self 2's computer, and it receives all the feedback it needs to accomplish the two prerequisites of winning in tennis: getting the ball over the net and into the court. This drill also keeps the mind so absorbed in the reality of the ball that it forgets to doubt, try hard, condemn or overinstruct itself because it is too occupied with the ball to interfere with Self 2's actions.

My experience with the "seeing the trajectory" exercise at Inner Game clinics has been rewarding. About 70 percent of the students find the exercise at least as absorbing as "bounce-hit." They become less judgmental about where they hit the ball and more aware of it as an object, and almost all of them report that that they move more easily toward the ball when they are simply "hooked on its curve" than when they are trying to get to it in position. Commonly, they speak of an effortlessness which surprises them; "It's as if someone else was hitting the ball" is a common remark. Rallies last a lot longer before the mind becomes self-conscious. One caution: sometimes students find lofty trajectories more aesthetically pleasing than lower arcs, and end up hitting a lot of lobs. This is fine for working on concentration, but it should be remembered that "trajectory" is primarily a trick; don't let Self 1 trick you back. Self 2 knows the most effective trajectories to hit in a match, so let it have its way.

The essence of the "bounce-hit" exercise was self-discipline, and required focusing the mind on reality: the ball and nothing else. The essence of "seeing the trajectory" and other related exercises is to find interest in *details*. The first step is to let go of one's normal concepts about something repetitious, to forget everything that one *thinks* one knows and allow the mind to find fresh interest. Aesthetics is not the *only* kind of interest—simply an example of one particular way that the mind finds to absorb itself.

Is the Ball a Moon?

One sunny day I was playing "seeing the trajectory" with a novice, and in the middle of a long rally Mary remarked, "Gee, the ball is really like the moon. Have you noticed that?"

When Mary said this, I thought that she was referring to the fact that the ball is in partial orbit over the earth, obeying the same laws of gravity as the moon.

"You mean it's like a small moon that doesn't make a complete orbit, but is attracted by earth's gravity?" I asked.

"No!" she said as if I had missed the most obvious thing in the world. "It has phases, just like the moon does."

This didn't make sense to me. The tennis ball was round, more like the sun; I'd never seen a crescent tennis ball. I looked puzzled, and Mary said in exasperation, "Look at the shadow!"

I looked again as we began another rally and was amazed. Part of the ball was in bright light, the other part in shadow —a quarter moon. That shadow had been on the ball every sunny day of my playing life, yet I had never really observed it. As I kept my eye and mind on the bright side of the ball, it absorbed my mind. Here was something I'd never seen simply because I hadn't been open enough to it—perhaps because I was too locked into the idea that a ball was round to be able to see the phases. More probably, I was simply too concerned with the pragmatic aspects of the ball to see the shadow.

Which is an important point. Often, in our attempt to be superefficient and notice only the practical, we miss a great deal of what is actually happening. In the long run this kind of concentration isn't practical because we lose interest, and results then suffer. Whatever aids our concentration, no matter how bizarre it may seem, is practical.

Gravity

One question I often ask a student doing the trajectory exercise is how a ball falls toward the court. Does it accelerate as it nears the ground, does it have a constant speed, or does it fall more slowly? You would be amazed at how many people have a hard time observing the answer to this question, especially if they've forgotten their high-school physics. To many the ball seems to fall at a constant rate, but of course it actually speeds up as it nears the court, and within a foot of the ground, both before the bounce and after, is at its greatest vertical speed. This is why it is so much more difficult to see at that instant than at the top of its trajectory, when it has very little vertical movement. This phenomenon explains why low volleys are so often mis-hit, and why half-volleys often can be hit with surprising power. Details, to be sure, but extremely practical ones. Gravity is so commonplace that we are usually oblivious to its effects on us and the ball.

Overcoming the "Ho-hums" off the Court

It's a psychological fact of perception that we only see what we're interested in. Of all the stimuli coming toward us at any given moment, we pay attention only to those that have meaning for us. To prevent an overload on our circuitry, we learn to block some parts of our experience. This is a natural, protective function of mind, but it can get out of control—or rather, in the control of Self 1, which has limited interests. When we start shutting off our receptiveness so much that we merely see, for example, a ball as "another backhand" or a man as "just another businessman," we limit our perceptions to the surface of our experience, and consequently are able to respond only superficially. The mind that skitters only on the surface is easily distracted, for it doesn't see enough detail or subtlety to hold its attention. Unable to remain focused on a single object or activity for long, it is unable to sustain interest in learning because it cannot penetrate the nature of things, where the real interest lies. When an entire culture loses its ability to find meaning in the commonplace, it becomes sick; its people become zombies unable to respond to stimulation other than those found in a variety of excesses, and it becomes harder and harder to have experiences which make them feel alive.

Letting Go of Concepts

The key to overcoming the "ho-hums" on or off the tennis court lies first, then, in recognizing that their cause is not primarily in the *event experienced*—the ball, the husband, the job, anything—but in the *mind of the experiencer.* It is not simply that certain events are inherently boring, but that the mind viewing them is programmed for boredom. We program ourselves for boredom whenever we think we already know *all* about something, whatever it is. Having seen so many tennis balls, we conclude that we know all about them. Our minds are so filled with concepts that we don't really observe. How often we see in a person, place or object only our own projections based on past experience. Regarding one's own static concepts over and over is what prevents our seeing things as they are, and this produces boredom. What we are actually doing is paying attention to our own *mental* creations, that is, our concepts, instead of to the event or object itself—to an unreal world instead of the real one—and we suffer the consequences.

Amnesia, or Practicing the Virtue of Ignorance

To help rid myself of the preconceptions which tend to rob me of the richness of present experience, I sometimes practice a game I call "amnesia," or "practicing the virtue of ignorance." Once again the game may sound a little strange to Self 1, but it has proven to be practical.

Try an experiment. Put down this book, shut your eyes for thirty seconds and listen to the sounds in the range of your hearing. Then, before reading further, tell yourself or someone else what you experienced. Perhaps you heard a passing car, people's voices, a noisy refrigerator or the sound of tennis balls. But did you *really* hear those sounds, or was it the *cause* of the sound that you heard? Self 1 tends to first react to sights and sounds by identifying and classifying them: "Yep, I know what they are. That's a refrigerator, that's a bird, that's a car." Next it makes judgments: "I like this sound, I don't like that one." That's generally all that is experienced: a classification and an ego reaction. There's not much there to really hold one's attention.

Now take a few seconds to relax, and then listen again. But this time pretend that you don't know what's causing the sounds and listen with your ears but with as little judgment or conscious thought as possible. Open yourself to the sounds that attract your attention and attend to their subtleties. When you have finished, compare the quality of this experience with the first. How long could you maintain an interest in pure sound when you forgot what you thought you knew?

I remember doing this simple exercise with my wife once driving home on the freeway. It was rush hour, and it looked as if we had a sixty-minute ride ahead of us. The gray roadside buildings looked their grayest through the already smog-darkened dusk, and our hearing was dominated by the noise of engines and tires on concrete. It was a dreary scene, one we had both suffered through countless times, but on this occasion we decided not to try to drown out these annoyances with the radio. Instead we attempted to really listen to what we heard, without identification, without thought or judgment, simply to perceive sounds as sounds, as changing patterns of frequencies.

I can't describe what we heard, but it was so interesting that we listened for an hour, conversing only briefly now and then to share our delight in what we were experiencing. This may sound hard to believe, and it may have been possible only because the practice of focusing our attention without any interference from the mind was not altogether new to us. But we both realized that if we could be content for an hour listening to the sounds of Los Angeles freeway traffic at dusk, with continued practice we would never have to fear boredom. The mind that can stay in the present and empty itself of its usual restless thoughts and reactions is one that can sustain interest and enjoyment amid the most common and repetitive phenomena, so it's worth a little effort to cultivate this discipline. It takes only a little practice to greatly increase one's awareness and enjoyment of the commonplace.

Consider this: Who is richer, a man with a million dollars to spend on enjoyable objects and places, or a man with the ability to enjoy himself wherever he is? We spend enormous effort on making our material circumstances more enjoyable, but wouldn't it be more efficient to expend that energy on increasing our innate abilities to find interest in our surroundings, whatever they are?

Forgetting My Wife

Sometimes I play a game called "I've never met my wife before." It is difficult but rewarding, and its object is to forget as many of the concepts—both negative and positive—that I have accumulated about Sally as I can. I try to forget I have ever seen her before. By this I don't mean that I act as I would when first meeting someone; rather, I simply let go of all the categories I hold in my mind about her, and when she says or does something I don't put what I hear or see into preconceived pigeonholes. When I succeed in this exercise, I am perceiving Sally in the present, and it's a fresh and lively experience. It's also hard to describe, but it's as different from my usual perception of her—from relating to her through the inevitable collections of thoughts, emotions and past impressions that one accumulates about people they see frequently—as day from night.

An example: Last night before going to bed, I asked Sally if she had turned down the heater. Already in bed, she replied, "No, I wasn't the last one in bed." I reacted with exasperation, thinking, There she goes again, assuming that I was criticizing her for not turning off the heater. Why does she always feel she has to defend herself? As I returned from turning down the thermostat, I said, "Boy, for a family who supposedly understands something about the Inner Game, we sure are sensitive to criticism."

Sally became annoyed at this remark, observing that it was *I* who was being sensitive to criticism. I couldn't see this. All I heard was continued criticism at a higher and higher pitch, and it became an uncomfortable scene. Finally I mustered control over myself and tried to listen to her. "Forget that she's your wife," I said to myself, "and listen to what this lady has to say." At first it was difficult, but slowly I was able to disentangle her words from all my past impressions and concepts of what she was "doing" to me once again, and simply listen to her.

I couldn't believe what I heard. It was the truth about myself. It was something I really needed to be told, but heretofore I hadn't let myself hear it from my wife. Self 1 was angry for a while, but soon had less control, whereas Self 2 was grateful and benefited immensely. When I looked at Sally now, she seemed entirely different. Actually, I believe that she became different the moment that I began to really listen to *her* rather than to my thoughts *about* her. What I perceived in her was an insight that I hadn't known was there, and that she really cared, even to the point of risking my disapproval and anger.

In retrospect, one of the most significant aspects of this transforming experience is that it started with something so commonplace.

A Man Who Let Go of His Preconceptions

A friend of mine named Bill told me once of an incident in which he practiced this kind of seeing. He was pretty advanced in the art—so much so that this story may sound incredible, but I tell it because it demonstrates the power that results from letting go of our concepts of what we think we know and letting Self 2 react naturally.

"I was sitting in a restaurant in my hometown with my family having lunch," Bill recounted, "when out of the corner of my eye I saw a man whom I knew slightly at the counter paying his bill. As the cashier was making change, I saw the man reach for a package of gum and put it in his pocket. My first thought was, I'm seeing something that no one else is seeing, and I immediately had the impulse to tell my family about it. But I resisted the impulse. 'What am I really seeing?' I asked myself. 'An example of injustice,' was my answer. My next thought was to tell the cashier, in order to make sure that justice prevailed. But again I found myself thinking, What am I really seeing? and this time the reply was, 'Honesty! I am understanding honesty by seeing what honesty is not! This act of dishonesty is showing me, by contrast, what honesty really is.'

"So clear was this perception, though so different from my normal way of thinking, that I got out of my chair, went over to the man with the gum in his pocket, put my hand on his shoulder and said in all sincerity, 'Thank you for showing me what honesty is.' As you might expect, the man was furious. He took the gum out of his pocket, slammed it down on the counter, picked up his change and stamped out the door."

Not knowing Bill, you may think this scene sounds a little crazy, but because he really had seen honesty and was grateful for the experience, it seemed logical to him to express his gratitude.

"Three days later I was in the same restaurant," Bill continued. "This time I was sitting alone when the same man who had taken the gum entered and came toward me. He asked if he could have a few words with me, and I invited him to sit down. 'Bill,' he said, "I want to tell you something about myself that no one else knows. For a long time I've been possessed by an irresistible impulse to steal. I have closets full of things at home, and I think my wife is beginning to suspect me. I don't know why I do it, but I can't seem to help it. What I wanted to tell you is that something very odd has happened. Ever since that incident in this restaurant last week, I haven't had the slightest urge to steal anything. I think it must have had something to do with what you said to me, and I'm grateful.' "

When I first heard Bill tell this story, I was very moved. My mind didn't really grasp the implications, but something within me responded strongly. Now I feel that I also understand a little with my mind as well. "Things like this happen to me quite often," Bill said, "but I'm always surprised."

Practicing the Virtue of Ignorance

This is another effective drill on the tennis court, but at first it is not easy to put into effect, for its basis is to forget how you played last time and to let go of any thoughts and expectations about how you will play today. I put all those thoughts—and there are often a lot of them—about how good or bad I think I am as a player right out of my mind.

Instead I muster the courage to "not know." I prefer this approach to either such positive or negative thinking as "I'm going to be terrific today," or "I doubt if I'll even be able to hit the ball over the net"—or anything in between. The reason is that when I can truly rid myself of any preconceptions, I become curious—and when I'm curious I'm really alert. Also, I haven't limited myself to any standard; regardless of whether I play well or badly, I'm surprised. When I'm not *afraid* to play poorly, inevitably the best comes out of me. The only time I really surpass myself is when I have a strong desire to play well, but at the same time feel that playing well or badly is equally satisfactory. This may sound contradictory, but it's true for me every time.

Progressing in the Art of Relaxed Concentration

Letting go of preconceived concepts, expectations and judgments—all the conscious thought of Self 1 that interferes with true perception—is difficult without constant practice in the art of relaxed concentration. Progression in this art is crucial to the winning of the inner game, or any outer game, for that matter, yet the word "concentration" is commonly misunderstood.

Once, after I had given a short talk to a group of players on the virtues of concentration and how to achieve it, a teaching pro remarked, "I hate to admit it, but to tell you the truth, I play less well when I'm concentrating than when I just go out and hit the ball." I appreciated this remark because it helped me to distinguish between what concentration is and isn't. What it *isn't* is trying to concentrate, or attempting to make yourself concentrate. How many times at college I remember trying to concentrate on a Shakespearean play the night before an English literature exam. The harder I tried, the less I understood and remembered; I was working so hard at *trying to concentrate* that I achieved very little reading or comprehension. Yet two days after the exam I could pick up the same play and become fully absorbed in it. I would appreciate what I was reading and it would stick with me.

So the teaching pro was right. Concentration in reading means that you read—and *nothing else.* Concentration in tennis means that you simply go out and hit the ball—and *nothing else. Trying* to concentrate is something quite different, for then we are paying attention not to the ball or the page but to our thoughts about how well we are concentrating, how much we are comprehending, how well or badly we are hitting the ball.

True concentration is the natural state of mind focused on the present, and it exists whenever the mind isn't wandering off into the past or future, or into the fantasy lands of what should or shouldn't, might or might not, be. The concentration of a child or an animal is an effortless focusing of attention on whatever is relevant in the present. It is only because our minds have become so restless and out of our control that it seems to take effort to achieve the state. But once we are truly concentrated we aren't even aware of it; we are focused only on the object or activity in which we are absorbed. There is no conscious effort to remain in the state; only after we are distracted is effort again required.

Four Stages in Relaxed Concentration

It could be said that there are four stages in entering into a state of relaxed concentration. The first could be called "paying attention," and it requires some degree of self-discipline. In order to pay attention to the words on this page, you must at least exercise the discipline of not looking at the pictures on the walls of the room, the television set and so forth. The "bounce-hit" and "mark the spot" drills are exercises that increase this self-discipline and make it possible to move easily into the second stage, which I call "interested attention."

The important thing to remember in this stage is not to strain. If you force it, your body will tighten along with your mind. So don't fight against yourself because the struggle will only distract you from the object of your concentration. When the mind is attracted by what it is paying attention to, you can be said to have achieved the stage of "interested attention." When you are interested in a good book, you don't have to *try* to concentrate because concentration becomes automatic. Sometimes I use the following example to differentiate between *paying* attention and achieving *interested* attention. If I were to look into my wife's eyes and say to her, "Sally, I'm trying hard to concentrate on you," realizing that this is hardly a complimentary remark she might reply, "Well, if you find it so hard to look into my eyes, go look somewhere else." But if I look into her eyes and become so absorbed that I say, "Sally, I can't take my eyes away from you," that's a different story. Sally realizes that I am really seeing her, and what I see is attracting my attention.

Thus, "absorbed attention" could be called the third stage of relaxed concentration. It is a difficult stage to describe, but its effect is that your attention becomes so riveted on what you are experiencing that it takes a very strong distraction to pull it away. Sometimes when I am absorbed in writing, the ring of the phone or the sound of children playing do not distract me in the slightest. When a person is truly absorbed in his tennis, nothing that a crowd or his opponent does can pull his attention away from the ball. A tennis photographer once told me that professionals who are playing well never seem to notice him taking pictures, but that as soon as one of them loses concentration and begins playing badly, he will complain about every click of the shutter.

Players doing the trajectory exercise often grow so absorbed in the ball's flight that not only are they difficult to distract, but they start seeing differently. It is not unusual for the ball to appear larger than it really is. I don't know why this happens, but I and a lot of others have experienced the phenomenon. A doctor I was teaching became so absorbed that afterwards he uneasily confessed that he thought he might be hallucinating because the tennis ball had seemed the size of a grapefruit. I reassured him that it was not hallucination but true perception, and that he should be grateful that because of its size the ball had been that much easier to hit.

Another common alteration of perception in states of absorbed attention is that the ball may appear to be traveling much slower. This phenomenon is not so difficult to explain. If we took a film with an old-fashioned movie camera of the flight of a ball moving forty miles an hour, when shown on the screen the ball might appear to be traveling sixty miles an hour for the same reason that Charlie Chaplin always seemed to walk double-time. Because the shutter speed of the older cameras was so slow, film was exposed to the ball only intermittently. Likewise, in our usual state of mind, even when we think we are looking at the ball, our eye is continually flicking away from it. But when the mind is absorbed in thoughtless concentration, there are no flicks; hence there is greater exposure and the ball "slows down." Professional baseball players have told me that when they are really hitting well, the ball actually appears to stop. I also know that in certain states of mind time seems to stop altogether. (This group of phenomena presents an interesting analogy to Einstein's theory of the relativity of time and space.)

The final stage in the process of relaxed concentration occurs when any sense of separation between oneself and a given experience is lost. This can be called "merging" or "a union" with experience, or simply "being wholly there." In this state there is no reaction or interpretation of the experience because the mind is completely still, causing a perfect reflection of the event as it really is. It is not possible to even attempt to describe this state, but those who experience it usually wish that they could be there all the time. It may be the only true seeing, a perception wholly free of the self-projections of Self 1. To encourage exploration of this kind of seeing, I recommend for the more adventurous Inner Game player an exercise called "riding the ball."

Riding the Ball

"Riding the ball begins after the mind has reached a high level of interest in the ball's trajectory," I told my friend Jim. "The mind follows the flight of the ball from one racket to the other, seeing it leave, then approach again, and there comes a point when you simply climb on it and 'ride' it as it flies through the air. You no longer see it leaving or approaching you because you are always with it. Instead of merely perceiving the ball, you feel gravity pulling you toward the court and the sharp change in direction as you bounce up toward the racket."

"Sounds hard," said Jim.

"It's hard to conceive, but not to experience at least partially. After becoming absorbed in the ball's trajectory, just climb on when you feel like it and stay on as if you're riding a horse. Don't let your mind fall off until the rally ends."

We exchanged several balls before either of us became concentrated. Then before I knew it I was on the ball feeling the air go by (windier on fast balls than on slow), feeling myself fly into the strings and springing up into the beginning of the trajectory. It was easy to tell when I stopped rising and I could sense when gravity began to exert its control to bring me down again. Time seemed to slow almost to a stop, and I was unconscious of running for the ball or swinging my racket. For a few moments I *was* the ball, and it seemed nearly perfect.

When the rally ended I turned to Jim. "How did it feel?"

"Scratchy!" he answered. "When I hit the net on that last shot, it was really scratchy." He laughed.

As I reread these lines, this incident sounds rather bizarre, but the experience is a distinctive one. I suppose the prosaic explanation is that all we were doing was imagining how it felt to be the ball; you could call it an exercise in empathy. All I know is that when I'm riding the ball, I *know* it better than when I am only watching it from a distance. I see it, feel it, hear it—and after a while it seems as if I *am* it.

When I get this far into the ball—it still doesn't occur whenever I want it to—it seems to be hit by an intelligence and a skill quite unfamiliar to me. The first time I managed to ride the ball in a match, I noticed that on several occasions I hit shots that I simply didn't know were in my repertoire. I also observed that in certain situations the ball went to spots where it had never before occurred to me to hit it. I had that same uneasy sense which seems to be characteristic of deep levels of concentration that someone else was making those shots. It's hard for the ego to take credit in these circumstances, but it certainly increases one's confidence in Self 2.

Unfocused Concentration. So far we have been speaking about attaining concentration by focusing on an object, the ball itself. In tennis this is a natural place to park the mind in order to keep it out of trouble, but in other sports and activities there may not be a single object which serves as a natural focus. In most team sports, for example, it is necessary to be concentrated but *un*focused, to be alert and present but not locked into any single object or event. But this kind of diffused concentration is also very effective in tennis, especially at more advanced levels. The mind is still concentrated in the present and is clear of all thought, but it is also open to the movement of other players and to other peripheral events. In most sports if you stop to think about what to do, you are too late. Seeing and response must follow one after the other without the interruption of thought. In skiing down a slalom course the eye can't focus on a single gate, but must be free to pick up, instant by instant, whatever relevant information it needs to negotiate all the turns. To me it's amazing that the human organism has the capacity to perform so precisely at such high speeds, but it's only possible with a quiet, alert mind.

Meditation

All the above ways of seeing the tennis ball—"bounce-hit," "seeing the trajectory," "art appreciation," "riding the ball"—could be called meditations of sorts. In its most general sense meditation simply means focusing one's awareness fully on some object, idea, activity or state of being. It is nothing more than pure concentration of mind. When we concentrate on the tennis ball, we are focusing on something external to our bodies but something actual. Certainly this is more calming to the mind than thinking about what might happen if you miss the ball. Calming the mind is an important goal of meditation, for when it is still, the eyes observe things as they are and understanding becomes automatic; whereas when the mind perceives the projection of its own fears and concerns, it becomes disrupted and distortion appears.

But, of course, there are drawbacks to using the ball as one's only object of meditation. The most obvious limitation is that eventually the point ends, and it would be a little ridiculous to continue watching the ball as it bounced and rolled to the fence. As a matter of fact, it is *after* the point is over that the mind becomes most vulnerable to distractions, for it is then that we are most apt to start thinking about the score and what will happen if we lose the next point. This is also when we become critical about past mistakes and start to visualize future ones. It can truly be said that most of the points in tennis are really lost when the ball is *not* in play. In between points and games is when the mind wanders and causes the misperceptions which increase errors when play resumes. Few players recognize sufficiently the importance of calming the mind and letting go of accumulated tensions during these brief periods of inactivity. A noteworthy exception is the example given by Arthur Ashe in the finals at Wimbledon in 1975. The television audience saw him sitting with his eyes shut and his head lowered, practicing stillness of mind. His victory over Jimmy Connors was one of the best examples I have ever seen of brilliant play with a minimum amount of interference from ego; Ashe's face looked exactly the same after a spectacular shot as it did after one of his few errors.

But the question remains: Where can I place my mind between points if not on the tennis ball? Many have found it possible to still their minds by using their breathing as an object of concentration. Focusing on the inhalation and exhalation of your own breath is one of the most ancient and natural forms of concentration. It keeps the mind on something actual which is always here and now, and it can be practiced in almost any situation to good effect. Because one's breathing is so intimately connected with life, placing our attention on it can increase our energy and bring us closer to our center. If observed without interference, the natural rhythm of the breath has the power to attract the mind and to reduce tension.

This exercise is simple, unobtrusive, effective if done attentively, and can be practiced anywhere and at all times. When practicing this form of concentration it is best not to consciously control your breath, but to allow it to find its own rhythm while your mind attends to it without interference.

Most forms of concentration, including listening to one's breath, a mantra, "bounce-hit," "seeing the trajectory" and the like, are confined to time and space and therefore are limited to the extent and duration they can quiet the mind.

Nonetheless, they can be most valuable because once a person has experienced the benefits of quieting the mind even a little, he becomes motivated to learn how to do it more completely. Eventually one grows to recognize that beneath the normal jabbering of the mind's thought processes something exists which is limitless and perfectly at peace. This part of ourselves has been called "pure consciousness," or, in my terminology, Self 3. By seeking and finding a practical way of connecting with that pure energy within, a person can repeat the experience at will; then, by using whatever skill he has in the art of relaxed concentration, he comes increasingly to know and identify with his essence. The closer a person comes to Self 3, or one's true center, the more capable he becomes of expressing his maximum potential as a human being. To enter into the fourth stage of concentration with that perfect energy within oneself can properly be called true meditation.

Two Shots or One Exchange?

Where does the power come from in a forehand drive? Self 1 would say that it emanated from our stroke or our transfer of weight. We tend to think that we produce the power of our shots, just as our opponent produces the power of his. But with the exception of the serve, this is not altogether true. Much of the power for what I call "my" forehand drive is already in the ball when it reaches me. The ball comes toward me with a certain force and direction, and what essentially happens when it meets my racket is that its direction is changed. After the serve, each player is simply redirecting the energy already in the ball and merely adding or subtracting a bit while he does so. I realized this fact one day when playing "riding the ball"; suddenly it appeared obvious that what had appeared as two separate shots, "mine" and "his," were really more a single exchange. The practicality of this insight soon became apparent. Instead of viewing the speed of the approaching ball as a threat, I began to welcome its energy. Realizing that there was no need to provide most of the power in a shot, I began using fewer muscles in my stroke; to achieve power what was mostly needed was a firm base from which to reflect the energy of the moving ball. My stroke used the smaller, more refined muscles to direct the ball and provide spin. Further, I realized that slow balls were not as easy as I had previously assumed; because they had relatively little energy, I had to provide more of my own energy. When I became more respectful of the difficulty of slow balls, I began to pay greater attention to them.

Can Self 2 Direct the Ball?

One day, while playing a set with another teaching professional, I introduced him to the awareness of using the power already in the ball, and was practicing this awareness exercise myself. He enjoyed the drill and said he was playing much better than usual, but admitted that a certain satisfaction was missing. "I liked thinking that *I* was providing the power," he admitted. "I also like the results of "letting go," as you call it, but I miss the sense that *I'm* doing the hitting." I remembered the dilemma of the lawyer in Chapter 1 and the frequent comments by Inner Game players that there is an entirely different kind of satisfaction involved in this mode of play. "I recognize that there is less satisfaction for the ego in playing this way," I said to the pro, "but see whether the kind of satisfaction which replaces it doesn't make up for it."

As we continued, a thought occurred which had never crossed my mind before. I realized that though I had trained myself to sabotage Self 1's sense of providing the power in the ball, I was still involved in *directing* it. In fact, in my first book, *The Inner Game of Tennis,* I even suggested that the proper role of Self 1 was to set the goal—that is, to decide where the ball should be hit—and then to be quiet and let Self 2 do it. But now I found myself thinking, What would happen if I didn't let Self 1 decide where to hit the ball, and allowed Self 2 to make the decision? If I don't consciously decide, at what point will I know where the ball is going to land? This so intrigued me that I decided not to choose where to place balls during the next two games.

The experiment was both exciting and illuminating. The first thing I discovered was that it was at about the moment my opponent's ball was passing over the net that Self 1 would decide where it wanted it to be hit. At that instant I could "hear" Self 1 directing me to hit cross-court or down the line. Instead of obeying, I waved the thought off. Then, as the ball bounced, a more urgent command would come, but I would wave this off as well. At some moment after my racket had begun swinging toward the ball and before the moment of contact, I knew where the ball was going to go. It wasn't a Self 1 decision; it was really precognition. And again and again the ball would land almost exactly where I thought it was going to. Even while serving, as my toss rose in the air I could hear my mind telling me where to aim, but it was only an instant before contact that I knew whether my shot would go down the middle or for the forehand or backhand corner.

What surprised me at first was the accuracy of all these shots. When I consciously aim, Self 1 always has its chance to help out and try to steer the ball a bit, and accordingly my shots are off target. But now I didn't even know where I was going to hit the ball until it was too late for Self 1 to interfere! It was the perfect method of bypassing the interference of my mind.

My second realization was even more startling. Not only were my shots more accurate, but they were usually placed exactly where my opponent wasn't. In fact, he almost always seemed to be on the side of the court where Self 1 had directed me to hit the ball as it was passing over the net. Both his Self 1 and mine had had similar ideas of where the ball should land, but Self 2 had different plans and fooled both me and my opponent. When I thought about this, it was easy to see why. My opponent would anticipate where I would hit my shot just as my Self 1 was deciding what to do, but because I was now delaying the decision longer than usual, he was anticipating too soon. Self 2 could see peripherally which way my opponent was leaning, and then would hit it in the other direction. Obviously, waiting until the last possible instant, when all the latest information was in and it was too late to interfere with the execution, was a far superior strategy. I wondered what would happen if I made other decisions in my life in the same way.

My final realization from this experience was that there

was a definite loss of a certain kind of satisfaction. Though my tennis was much better than normal, now Self 1 wasn't getting any credit whatsoever. Previously I had excluded it from the stroke and the power, and now even the direction was beyond its control. Self 1 really wasn't needed at all. At the same time I felt another kind of satisfaction, one of almost complete self-expression. I felt both sad and full simultaneously. I wasn't sure whether I would continue this exercise or not, but one thing was certain: the tennis was my very best, and there was absolutely no boredom.

4
Feeling the Difference: An Introduction to Body Awareness

The essence of the Inner Game learning process can be summed up in two words: *increasing awareness.* Awareness is what gives us the feedback from experience, which is our best teacher. In tennis two major kinds of feedback are necessary: a primarily visual feedback from the flight of the ball; and bio-feedback, from the movement of the body.

The last two chapters dealt with our sense of *seeing,* and encouraged the art of observation, whether of a tennis ball or any other object or event. This chapter is about *feeling,* and how to increase awareness of the body and racket while they are in motion. Heightening our ability to feel what is happening within our own muscle system is the key to the refinement of every athletic movement, and is transferable to most other activities in our lives.

Body Awareness

What is body awareness? The best way to make the meaning of this phrase clear is to experiment with getting in touch with your own body. For example, here is a simple exercise. Raise your right hand over your head. Now lower it. Now raise your hand a second time, but this time focus on how it feels as you are lifting it. In other words, increase awareness of your hand rising in the air. Then experience your hand lowering again. What was the difference between the two sets of movement? Now lift your arm a third time, this time with your eyes shut so that you can pay fuller attention only to *feeling*. How can you tell that your arm is actually moving? What sensations indicate the location of your arm at each moment? Can you distinguish between the sensations telling you that your arm is moving upwards from those of the downward movement? If you are paying close attention you can feel some muscles tightening while others relax at the moment the arm changes direction and descends. Can you locate the muscles which contract in order to raise the arm, and can you feel them let go as the arm lowers?

Subtle, isn't it. The more attentive and relaxed the mind, the more able it is to pick up increasingly minute muscle and energy sensations in the body. This exercise may be continued with other parts of the body, increasing your body awareness each time. The more attentive the mind grows, the subtler the sensations it can pick up. The more delicate the sensations the mind attends to, the calmer and more aware of still more refined sensations it becomes.

In all my years of playing tennis, basketball, football and golf at school or college, no coach ever showed me how to become aware of my own body. They were more interested in how many times I was able to perform a given exercise, as in calesthenics, or in explaining the proper form of an action. I was always too busy trying to do something "right" to really feel what my body was doing. It wasn't until I took a class in hatha yoga when I was thirty-three years old that an instructor encouraged me to become aware of the sensations of my arms, legs and body when in movement. It was a tremendously exciting shock. My teacher really seemed more interested to know if I was experiencing my body's movement than if I were doing the postures correctly. I was stunned by how quickly, under this emphasis, I learned the proper form. When I translated this awareness into tennis and into my teaching of it, there were dramatic improvements in both.

Achievement through Awareness

In our culture relatively little importance has been given to body awareness. The emphasis is on achievement rather than on awareness. Yet it is only those athletes who have a highly developed kinesthetic sense—muscle sense—who ever achieve high levels of excellence. One simply can't play any sport well lacking the ability to focus carefully on the subtle body sensations which indicate the difference between balance and off-balance, timing and mis-timing, too tight and too loose. Body awareness is directly related to body achievement.

In the Japanese and Chinese cultures most children are introduced to one form or another of the martial arts, and all of these place great emphasis on alertness to subtle body sensations. In tai chi chuan, the best known of the Chinese disciplines, every movement is made with careful slowness to increase awareness, not only of the subtlest muscle movements but also of the even more delicate flows of energy throughout the body. Once this awareness is mastered, a tai chi or aikido master possesses amazing levels of competence, though not so much by chasing achievement as by pursuing increased awareness. Achievement is the inevitable and natural by-product of awareness.

The will to strive for higher and higher levels is also necessary, and has been the greatest spur to the development of sport in the Western world. But I believe that we have overstressed our emphasis on achievement, and that a rebalancing in the direction of awareness is needed. Pure awareness, with little will to achieve, lacks direction, but the will to achieve with too little awareness is strained and lacks the requisite refinement to attain the highest levels of excellence.

The human body is a magnificent instrument that is constantly sending us subtle messages which, if heard and heeded, would keep us healthy and operating at the highest levels of efficiency. But when we become too goal-oriented and excited about the results of our actions, we begin to lose touch with our bodies. Lacking awareness of its messages, ultimately our performance suffers.

Awareness Is Not Thinking

Before beginning an exploration of ways to increase our body awareness on or off the court, a clear distinction must be made between *awareness* and *thinking*. Often when I ask a student to become aware of his body while he is serving, he replies, "What do you want me to think about?" But to be aware does not mean "to think about." Rather, it means to experience something directly, whereas to think means to have a thought *about* what you are experiencing. They are two different processes. The more one thinks about an experience, the less aware he becomes of the experience itself. Awareness increases as thinking decreases. If, for example, I am listening to a person who is talking to me, and I observe his face and attend his words, I will be aware of the communication between us. But if, while he is speaking, I am thinking, I wonder how he feels about me, or I don't agree at all with what he is saying . . . how can I convince him that he's wrong when I get a chance to speak, I am obviously going to lose awareness of the communication occurring at that moment.

Likewise, after a person executes a stroke, I commonly ask, "What did you experience?" Frequently the answer comes back in terms of what *wasn't* experienced, as in "I didn't turn sideways," "I'm not following through," or "I'm not watching the ball." All of these are thoughts *about* what was experienced—that is, facing the net throughout the stroke, or stopping the follow-through in midswing. If I ask, "How do you know you didn't watch the ball?" the answer may be "Because I hit it on the wood."

"How do you know?" I persist.

"Because I felt my whole arm vibrate when I hit the ball."

"Aha! *That's* the experience: your arm vibrated. Everything else you said was merely thoughts about *why* it vibrated."

Thinking about an experience separates one from the experience itself. Awareness decreases as thinking increases.

The same applies to one's tennis stroke. If while serving I am thinking, I must remember to break my elbow and let my racket fall down my back, reach up high, make sure to snap my wrist . . . uh-oh, my toss is too far behind me, I'd better come over the top of the ball or I'll hit it out, there will be little awareness of the kind demonstrated in the arm-raising exercise; most of the subtle sensations of muscle movements, balance, rhythm and timing will be lost. The more we think about what we are doing, the more we lose the feel of it. Feeling is a direct experience—no thinking is required—and every athlete knows that when he loses the feel of what he's doing, he's in trouble. Remember how easy it was when you were a child to learn how to ride a bicycle. It took feeling and balance, not thinking.

Yoga Tennis: An Exercise in Body Awareness

Increasing your body awareness is a matter not of philosophy but of practice, so let's practice a little body awareness with a racket. (If you don't happen to have one around, use the palm of your hand.) Let your body swing a forehand stroke while you put your attention on your movements. Swing very slowly so that you can catch as many subtle sensations as possible. *Experience* the path of your racket from start to finish, noticing with your kinesthetic sense the exact shape of the path your racket carves in space. Do this several times, becoming more attentive with each stroke.

Did you find yourself thinking about whether you were swinging the racket correctly? Or were you trying to guide it in order to maintain your concept of good form? If so, you have missed much of what was really happening. Swing again, but this time make no effort to control the path, and continue until it feels as if the racket were taking itself back. Let go of all judgments about your stroke; simply let your racket swing itself, without any help from you. Meanwhile, focus all your attention on the swing without any effort to change it; just feel it, wherever it goes. Do this until you can tell the difference between when you are *trying* to swing the racket a certain way, and when you are simply observing it. When this distinction is clear, and not just intellectually—that is, when you can sense the difference between *controlling* and *feeling*—you have grasped the key to excellence in all body-movement skills.

Should versus Is

The primary obstacle to body awareness is our tendency to conceive our actions in terms of "good" and "bad." It is virtually impossible to become truly aware of a tennis stroke, for example, when you feel that it is "bad," "wrong" or "uncoordinated." Test this out. Take a slow-motion swing with your best stroke, the one you like the most; then take another swing with what you consider your worst. In which was it easier to focus on the path of the racket? In which did you experience more?

One of the most difficult moments in teaching racket awareness is when the student is sure that his racket is in the wrong place. Convinced that it is too high, he has a hard time feeling how high it actually is. If he believes that there is an uncoordinated hitch in his swing, he won't really feel the hitch. The Inner Game professional has to help his pupil rid himself of judgment in order to allow the feedback from the body to be experienced. He may say, "Yes, that hitch is really there, but that's okay, let's not try to change it. Simply focus on it the way it is right now." Only when his judgment stands aside can the player feel this "horrible" action as it truly is. Once he experiences it, he can then detect when it is greater and when smaller, and easily gain control of it.

In inner tennis this principle of nonjudgmental awareness is of paramount importance. In essence, the point of the game is to meet a moving ball with a moving racket. The ball is seldom where it *should* be, but it is *always* where it *is*. Similarly, one must hit the ball that *is* with a racket that *is*. The racket that "should be" will miss the ball that "is." "Should" and "is" are incompatible because they are in different dimensions. Therefore, it is more important to pay attention to where your racket is than to be constantly worrying about where it should be. "But if I don't take my racket back when I should, something bad will happen," intrudes the thinking, controlling Self 1.

Test this notion thoroughly before believing it. Even if you succeed in taking your racket back to where it should be, if you have no sense of where it *is,* the shot won't happen. But if you know where your racket is, even if it's not the "correct" position, Self 2 will still have a chance to make an effective shot. The priority of *is* over *should* is fundamental to the Inner Game approach.

In the following pages we will explore how increasing awareness of what *is* leads automatically toward greater effectiveness. With increased awareness of *is, should* soon follows. Beneficial change is merely a natural by-product.

Racket Awareness

Focus again on your racket as you swing. Consider the racket an extension of your own arm and attempt to develop a feel for this longer limb. If you shut your eyes it may help you to experience the sensations that tell you of the location of your racket during its path. Then, at the moment your racket is fully back—that is, the instant before it begins its forward movement—hold it steady in position. Don't look at it; simply feel where it is. With eyes closed, imagine what the racket looks like. Imagine the level of its head in relation to your waist and shoulders, the angle of its face (flat, open or closed), and its angle to the rest of your arm. When you have these three elements clearly pictured, open your eyes and take a look. Were there any surprises? To what extent was your racket exactly where you thought it was? Continue the exercise until there is little or no difference between where you feel your racket to be and where in fact it actually is.

As you continue to experience your racket, letting it move itself, as it were, do you notice any changes taking place? Has the position of it changed? Do your muscles feel different as you move your arm? Notice the direction of these changes, but don't allow Self 1 to interfere by saying, That feels better so I must make sure to keep doing that. Merely allow any alteration to take place until it stops. The same intelligence which guided those changes knows, by feeling and by observing the results, when they should stop. The more a player trusts this intelligence, the more he learns how worthy of trust it really is.

Now turn your attention to your lower body and concentrate on your balance and shifting weight. Again, don't *try* to shift your weight; simply notice whatever sensations occur in your body when you shift your balance during the stroke. Don't try to stay balanced, but notice the different sensations of balance and imbalance. Allow your body to move the way it wants to, and let go of any imposed control. Be curious about whatever is happening. How do the knees bend? The ankles? How does the torso twist, if at all? When you have increased your awareness of the legs and torso, allow your stroke to resume its normal speed and focus your awareness on your body as an entity. Experience the rhythm and feel of your stroke as a single movement.

This same kind of awareness can be practiced with each stroke, slowly at first, noting all sensations and changes attentively, and then retaining the same level of awareness as you swing at normal speeds. By drilling in this manner, you can greatly increase the awareness of your strokes as they truly are, and beneficial changes will begin to occur automatically. Thereafter, the only task is to learn to attain the same high level of awareness when a ball is approaching you, first while rallying, then during a practice match, and finally in the middle of an important point during a crucial match. Your body is always sending you important messages, no matter what the situation; it's your choice as to what extent you receive them clearly.

Awareness versus Trying

To repeat: the key to increased awareness of your body and swing lies in your willingness to relax your conscious *control* over what you are doing. Awareness is inversely proportional to our attempts to control our actions by our minds. To the extent to which we let go of this inferior control—Self 1—natural learning takes place and the body is motivated by a far more sophisticated process. Once again we are confronted with that age-old truth which so agonizes

Self 1: to gain control, you first must let go of it. Or spelling it out in pragmatic tennis terms: to keep the ball in the court, you must stop trying so hard to do so.

Shifting the center of control from Self 1 to Self 2 is the heart of the Inner Game process, and it begins and ends with the simple practice of increasing your awareness. Performing these exercises in front of a mirror can heighten your awareness of your stroke by giving you *visual* feedback along with the kinesthetic feedback from your muscles. (Note: Mirrors don't judge; only the mind evaluates what the mirror reflects. When our minds themselves act like perfect mirrors, we have won the Inner Game.)

Body Awareness off the Court

Of course, there are many ways to increase awareness of your body in movement besides exercises with a tennis stroke. As I've mentioned, my own first explorations into this art took place as a novice in hatha yoga. If taught competently, classes in aikido or tai chi chuan or other martial arts can lift one from only a superficial awareness of one's body and energies to an extremely sophisticated level. I would recommend these disciplines to anyone who wants to increase his excellence in any sport, particularly because they will do much more than sharpen his skill in performing a particular movement. They also increase your ability to be aware, therefore to learn, and to enjoy movement and appreciate your body. Finally, they develop both the skills and the thirst necessary for greater self-knowledge, the ultimate goal of these ancient disciplines.

Besides such formal methods there are unlimited other ways to increase awareness of one's body in motion, and most of them can be practiced at any time. For instance, if you are sitting at this moment, you can practice focusing on it. Scan your body; do you feel comfortable? Is there any tension in your back, neck or shoulders which you hadn't previously been aware of? If so, let your body move into the position it wants to be in for reading. Don't make it conform to any preconception of correct posture, but by keeping attentive to how it feels, allow it to find its own best bearing.

If your posture doesn't change, and you are not holding it with Self 1, you can safely assume it is already in its natural posture.

Walking or Jogging. What a difference there is between merely walking to get somewhere and being aware of your body while walking, or between jogging simply for exercise and focusing on your sensations while doing so. Running while fully aware of running is a wonderful experience. Let the body decide what pace to set and the length of stride; simply let go while you are carried along for the ride. Self 2 finds its own rhythm. It knows when to slow down and when to break through the limit you had set in your mind. Only by trusting your body to lead you is it possible to discover its innate intelligence. You can learn everything you need to know about the joy and technique of running by paying attention to your body as it moves.

Abandoned Control

Running down a Mountain. Shortly after graduating from college, I climbed a mountain above Montreux in Switzerland. The route was mostly over broken rock and was not difficult, but it took longer to reach the top than I had expected, and by the time I was ready to turn back, sunset was only two hours away. I began running down the mountain, more or less jumping from one boulder to the next, hesitating each time while I looked for the next rock, trying to make sure that I didn't catch an ankle between rocks and that I didn't build up too much speed and lose control. But I still wasn't making good enough time. Goaded by the need to get down before dark, I abandoned caution and moved faster and faster. Soon I was running too fast to consciously pick out the next rock. My feet were finding their own landings faster than I could think about them. At first this was quite frightening, but when I saw that my body always found a safe target as long as I merely kept my eyes open and let go, it became an exhilarating experience. I forgot my fear and became intently aware only of my body and the mountain beneath me. It was one of the first times that I had experienced the control that results from really letting go. I've never forgotten the experience, but it was a long time before I connected it to the playing of tennis or other sports, or to life in general.

Driving a Car. While driving a car on a freeway or in the midst of city traffic, it is possible to observe the distinct difference between the exercise of Self 1's and Self 2's control. Most of us generally employ Self 2 control while driving, but when Self 1 dominates you can feel the tension and tiredness accumulate in your shoulders.

Driving also shows us the proper relation between having a goal and being aware of the here and now. When you step into your car with the intention of driving home, it isn't necessary to keep reminding yourself to remember to go home; instead, you simply pay attention to what is happening in front of you, respond appropriately without thinking and arrive home without tension. On the other hand, if you are constantly worrying about getting home on time or getting lost, you are apt to miss what is happening in the present and never make it home.

Sex. A good example of the loss in experience which comes from trying too hard for results occurs in the bedroom. If a person is overly concerned about achieving a certain preconceived result for himself or for his love partner, he may not realize the fullness of the experience. Worry and doubt about what might not happen dulls the feelings that *are* happening. If a person is unable to be wholly alive to a simple touch and appreciate it for itself, he will not reach the climax of feeling that those simple touches were preparations for. A great deal of sex therapy focuses on this simple point. Feel what you feel; let go of judgment; let the results take care of themselves.

The same insensitivity to feeling can be produced by over-instruction in sex. A person who is too intent on technique won't be able to experience subtleties of feeling and consequently will miss a large part of the enjoyment he seeks. Just like tennis, the sexual act requires surrender to the wisdom of the body if your full potential is to be realized. It requires leaving your mind, worries and attachments, and literally coming to your senses. When this state is achieved, the senses become governed by a superior intelligence that is innate in every human and that allows for the full expression of one's identity at one's present stage of development. The beauty of such action is self-evident; it is simple and spontaneous, and markedly different from behavior born in self-doubt and premeditation. Once the mind grows involved in worrying and trying, it becomes exceedingly difficult to find one's way back to the simple experience of a touch, or to tell the difference between affection and greed.

Diet. It seems to me that one of the most obvious indications that modern man has lost touch with the wisdom of his own body is the number of books written and bought on diet and nutrition. There are literally thousands of books on the best way to take off weight, and thousands more on maintaining health by eating the "right" foods. But the authority for this "right" is usually placed squarely in the hands of the author of the book. Few think to ask the body itself what it needs, or to even check by direct experience whether a given diet works for them or not. Once again Self 1 intrudes; it reads the books and then plays the role of know-it-all, while the body is regarded either as stupid or as simply wanting what isn't good for it.

Yet experiments with young children offered a free choice of food in a cafeteria show that after a given period of time (needed, I imagine, to overcome a natural inclination to indulge in all those externally imposed shouldn'ts) the children selected nutritious and well-balanced meals without any outside help. It is doubtful that the same results would be obtained by adults, since most have largely neglected their ability to discriminate between the hungers of the body and those of the mind. Adults eat to assuage their loneliness, to distract them from worry, or to rebel against moral impositions, and none of these motives are apt to result in diets which meet the needs of the body. Even if we decide to eat according to the criteria of what is nourishing, we feel lost without consulting an external authority to tell us exactly what our diet should be. We have become entirely dependent on labels and prescriptions; "How am I supposed to know what's good for me?" we ask with innocent bewilderment. At least a partial answer to this question is simple: by paying closer attention to your body. Although I haven't made a thorough study of the problem, there is no doubt in my mind that all of us are capable of becoming much more sensitive to the signals from our body which tell us when it is ingesting what it needs and when it isn't. At the very least we could receive enough feedback from our insides to notice when a given diet is helping or hurting us. I don't mind receiving advice from doctors or others with wider experience, but I don't like being totally dependent on an outside authority for diagnosis, prescription and results.

One day, Molly—the same overweight Molly who had received her first tennis lesson on television—approached me and asked, "How about applying the Inner Game to dieting? Would it work?" I hesitated to answer because I didn't feel I had sufficient experience. "Molly, the more I eat, the skinnier I seem to get. I really don't think I can help."

But Molly insisted that I give her at least a theoretical interpretation of how Inner Game principles would apply to diet. On the theoretical level it was easy. "Inner Game practice is based on increasing awareness, so in dieting one should focus on increasing awareness of your body and of food." We discussed how one might become attuned to what and when the body wanted to eat, as opposed to the promptings of the mind. We also talked about paying careful attention to the sensations of the body during and after each meal. For example, how do you really know when you've had enough? Can you feel your stomach having trouble digesting certain foods? What difference does the order of eating make? Or the speed? How long does your body want to chew different foods? "Observations of these and other points, plus attending to the inclinations of the body, may give the feedback necessary to discover an intelligent diet for yourself," I suggested. "At least it wouldn't hurt, and you might learn something from the experiment."

A month later Molly returned fifteen pounds lighter and looking very well, so I asked her about her experiment.

"I did my shopping in the supermarket by just walking down the aisles and noticing all the different foods. I let my arm reach for whatever I felt my body needed. I let go of all preconceptions about what was good for me, what I liked, and what was fattening, and told my body that it could have anything it really wanted. I was amazed at the results. I chose foods that I had hardly ever eaten before. For example, for almost two weeks straight my body chose to have cabbage for dinner, a dish I haven't had more than a few times in my entire life. Perhaps there was something in cabbage that I really needed, but after those two weeks I haven't chosen it again."

Molly told me also that she hadn't forced herself to stop eating during any meal, but had simply paid attention to an inner signal telling her when she'd had enough. She ate some food she thought was fattening, but allowed herself to do so without recrimination. Occasionally she had experienced some difficulty in discriminating between what her body wanted and what her mind wanted and in ignoring what her mind said that her body needed. But often it was easy to make this distinction because the body generally seemed to know what it wanted.

"Do you think you'll end up with the figure you want?" I asked.

"Well, maybe, or maybe not," Molly answered. "I suspect that Self 1 and Self 2 have different ideas about my figure as well as my tennis. I think that perhaps I can live with the kind of figure that Self 2 will guide me to."

Does Nonjudgmental Awareness Work?

How can I expect increasing awareness of my stroke to bring about the necessary improvements I'm looking for? Won't I simply increase my awareness of my mistakes? This is the basic doubt of most people who undertake to practice nonjudgmental awareness. The belief that has to be overcome is that if you don't make yourself play correctly and try to eradicate your errors, you will continue to hit the ball wrong and won't improve.

This is exactly what Self 1 would like you to believe. "Body," it says in effect, "you are hopeless without my constant help. Without me you'll never get better; you really need me." The fundamental Inner Game experiment is to test whether this hypothesis is true. We can experiment by letting go of as much Self 1 control as we can, allowing the body do its own thing while becoming increasingly aware during the process. Let go and then see what happens. I don't believe that anyone becomes really convinced that the body will self-correct until he has experienced it happening a number of times.

Let's return to the tennis court and use a specific example. Take a player whose forehand is erratic because the pitch of his racket face is so open at the moment of contact that most of his shots sail out of the court. If a teacher tells this player that his racket is too open, it won't do much permanent good unless the student actually experiences what his racket feels like when it is open and when it is flat. If he simply believes the teacher and tries to correct the flaw by telling himself to close his racket, it will soon be too closed. At first he will find his forehand improving. I should remember to close my racket face a little, he will say to himself. But after his racket is flat, he is still apt to be reminding himself to keep it that way, and soon he will return for another lesson because his tennis isn't working. Though it may produce initial, temporary success, using verbal cues to control one's strokes usually ends up not working. Yet many players, even at advanced levels, keep looking for the latest tip to improve or correct their stroke.

The alternative way of dealing with the open racket face is to learn to distinguish the difference between a slightly open face and a flat one by becoming attuned to the muscles in your wrist and hand. Putting your attention on the subtle difference in feeling, and perceiving the resulting trajectories, give the brain the nonverbal information it needs to correlate the variables of racket-face openness with these trajectories. The necessary correction then takes place automatically.

None of this is magic. The human brain is an extraordinarily sophisticated learning instrument capable of making distinctions between movements on a much more subtle level than our verbal language is capable of. It learns that on some balls, for instance, a slightly open racket is effective, and that on others a slightly closed face produces the desired results. It can regulate the difference by no more than half a degree and know just when to use it. Our conscious thinking mind has nowhere near this level of control over our bodies.

This example is not so much a support of a new learning theory as a description of how learning takes place. Even a player who uses a lot of verbal instructions in an attempt to control his body's movement actually learns by the only way he can: by awareness of the ball and his body. Without getting some kinesthetic feedback from the body, it would be impossible to return a single ball. No one can effectively think his way through a single tennis stroke; it's simply too complicated. We learn by feedback, and experience is our only true teacher. It is our ability to tune into this experience which makes all the difference between effective and ineffectual learning.

Muscle Memory

In Chapter 1 it was suggested that there could be no learning without memory. By "memory" I do not mean conceptual memory, nor even memories which can be recalled at will. Learning complex sets of motor skills such as those needed in tennis is possible only by using the memory of past sense-experiences on the court. These sense-experiences are collected and collated in such a way that our responses become increasingly organized and efficient. This is true regardless of whether we have ever conceptualized this learning. Thus, learning in tennis is the result of the connection and retention of the primary events in the game: the movement of the ball and the movement of the body. Visual images of trajectories are collated with the kinesthetic images —the muscle memory—of the body's response. There is really no other way for it to happen. The organism learns that it can obtain a specific muscle result by inducing a certain complex pattern of movements. Seeing a ball of a particular speed and trajectory approaching, it remembers that in the past a certain series of movements produced a shot of a particular speed and trajectory in response. This is a very complex process and yet a very effective one which in contrast makes the verbal instructions of Self 1 look primitive indeed.

Bio-Feedback

The process of learning the motor skills outlined in this chapter is similar to that described in bio-feedback experiments. These have demonstrated that a man can learn to control the rate of his heartbeat, his blood pressure or other such so-called involuntary bodily processes simply by being hooked up to a device which offers him feedback from the organ to be controlled. If an amplified signal which corresponds to his blood pressure is beamed into a person's ear, he can learn to raise or lower his blood pressure at will in a very short time. He exerts this control not by learning a concept or by being told what to do, but simply by hearing the differences in the changes in sound. The promises of this kind of learning for maintaining health are enormous. Inner Game learning takes place in the same way, but without an external amplifier. The player simply amplifies the feedback from his body by calming his mind and thereby increasing his awareness of bodily signals. Some techniques that help to do this more easily will be discussed in the following chapter.

5
Ways of Cooperating with Natural Learning in Tennis

Once a person can experience the difference between forcing an action and letting it happen, between Self 1 controlling his movements and Self 2 being allowed to take control, a preference gradually develops. He comes to realize that his play is more effortless and effective when his thinking ego-mind is out of the way and his body can learn and perform without interference.

But recognition of the practical superiority of Self 2, even if it grows out of experience rather than belief, does not necessarily mean that the player will at once stop interfering with his full potential.

The Inner Game method of learning is not a new theory, but simply a natural way of cooperating with the way that learning always takes place. Self 1 can interfere with natural learning or decide to cooperate with it. It can interfere by trying to take over a function that it can't perform well, such as giving instructions to the body's muscles; it can cooperate by staying calm and paying enough alert attention. The Inner Game is the practice of quieting the mind and overcoming whatever obstacles prevent the best that is within us from expressing itself.

Still, to realize practical benefits one must practice effective methods. Knowing the techniques of the inner game and understanding how and why they work can be interesting and illuminating, but in the long run only practice will increase lastingly one's level of understanding. The purpose of this chapter is to introduce the reader to some methods of increasing body awareness which I have found helpful, not merely as explanations of principles, but as tools that can help a player make continual progress in the developing of Inner Game skills. Though these methods were developed on the court and therefore seem to relate mostly to tennis, it is not difficult to extrapolate them to fit many other activities. Behind every technique is one principle: improvement is facilitated by increasing awareness of what *is*. There are unlimited ways of doing this, and it's easy and fun to invent new games which increase your awareness. Those which work the best for you are the ones you will stick with until they have served their purpose.

Increasing the Racket Awareness of a Beginning Student

Chapter 2 described how to help a beginner by increasing his awareness of the ball. Here is an example of how the learning process can be continued with an emphasis on body awareness.

Mary comes to the court for her first lesson. She has never held a racket in her hand before and looks a little apprehensive. "I used to play golf," she begins. "I took a lot of lessons but never became very good. Finally it got so frustrating that I gave it up. That was quite a few years ago, and I haven't played any sports since. But now my husband has become a tennis addict, and I've decided that if I want to see him on weekends I'd better learn the game."

Listening to Mary, it's easy to see that she's already set herself up. Because of her past experience with golf, she doubts her ability to learn, and yet at the same time she wants to be playing tennis with her husband within a few weeks.

High expectations and a lot of self-doubt—the perfect conditions for trying too hard and a lot of frustration.

I begin by asking Mary to swing her racket around a little without looking at it, just to get used to how it feels. "With a racket in your hand you have a longer arm than before, so become familiar with it."

Soon I start bouncing a ball on the court with my racket and ask her to do the same. As she starts she is already tight, trying to make sure that she hits the ball every time.

"It doesn't matter if you hit it," I say. "I only want you to observe how the seams spin as the ball comes up to meet your racket. Do they spin once? Twice? Half a spin? Just watch."

Immediately Mary's motion begins to smooth out and she hits the ball on the strings without trying.

"Now bounce a few in the air, like this, still keeping your eyes on the seams. It's okay to miss."

Mary does this for a couple of minutes. She misses a few, but is unconcerned.

Many pros use this exercise to teach children and other beginners, because it is simple and develops hand-eye coordination. With every hit, Self 2's memory bank is automatically accumulating information about the length and weight of the racket, the location of the strings in relation to the handle, and so forth. In the same way that a newborn baby doesn't know where his hand is and can't grab an object until he has experimented a little, a beginning player doesn't really know where the strings of his racket are, and should not be asked to hit a ball with it until he has had the chance to become familiar with its feel.

Within a few minutes Mary learns a great deal about where her racket head is, the effect that its angle has on the flight of the ball, the difference between the sounds of balls hit by the center of the face and those mis-hit near the frame, and much more. But perhaps most important is that she begins the game without the stress of having her achievement measured. In fact, I often start a lesson with a beginner by volunteering never to ask her to do anything she won't be able to achieve. All that is expected of her is to observe a ball and feel a racket. So far, no judgments, no criticism, no compliments, merely experiencing whatever happens.

Now Mary is ready for the "bounce-hit" exercise described in Chapter 2. Again, before she is asked to hit the ball, she learns to see it and to become aware of different speeds and trajectories as it approaches. I listen to the tone of Mary's voice as she says "Bounce" and "Hit." Seeing the ball coming toward her is different, and anxiety tightens her throat. When she does hit it, the tightness is also expressed by her body and makes contact difficult. But eventually the voice that says "Hit" is as calm as the one that says "Bounce," and she is making good contact with most balls and has overcome a lot of self-doubt. Still, though she is now calm and focused on the ball, her swings are understandably erratic. Sometimes the racket is taken back in a high arc and comes slicing down through the ball; at other times the face is open and comes from below, lobbing the ball way out of the court. Because there is a huge variation in swing there is much variation in the results. On the other hand, her footwork on both backhand and forehand is nearly perfect, though totally unconscious, and she is seeing the ball well, making contact and, most important, experiencing no frustration.

I decide to take Mary's attention off the bounce-hit of the ball and focus it on her body and racket. "You can stop saying "Bounce-hit" now. I want to shift your attention from the ball to your racket. See if you can gradually become more aware of the path your racket is carving in space as it swings back and then toward the ball."

At this, Mary again looks slightly apprehensive. Her next three strokes are considerably tighter and more jerky, and on two of them the ball hits the frame of the racket. I surmise that she's remembering all her frustration in trying to swing a golf club correctly. I imagine that she is also experiencing the universal problem with body awareness: now that her attention is on her body, she is sure there's something wrong with what she is doing and that I'm trying to correct her. She begins trying to correct herself, and therefore tightens even more.

"I want you to begin to notice the level of your racket at the back of your swing," I say without disapproval.

"Where should it be?" Mary asks anxiously.

"Just where it is, for right now," I answer. "But where is it? Can you feel it back there?" Mary looks at me suspiciously; she thinks I'm tricking her. She doesn't believe that her racket is where it should be and wonders why I won't tell her the right position so that she can at least try to swing it correctly. I throw her a few more balls. "Well?" I ask.

"I think I was taking it back too high, right?" she asks eagerly.

"Perhaps, but for right now 'too high' is okay. Just let it go there without trying to change it," I reassure her. "What I'm really interested in at this moment is whether you can actually tell its exact position."

"Well, I think I'm taking it back about shoulder height, right?" she asks tentatively. Actually, on her last three shots, her racket has gone back well above the level of her head.

"Check it out and make sure," I say, throwing her a few more balls. After a little coaxing of this kind, Mary forgets about trying to hit the ball over the net. The tension leaves her mouth, her forehead is relaxed, and her stroke is a lot less jerky.

"On that last shot, my racket was right here!" she declares affirmatively, putting her racket about six inches over her head and behind her back to show me the spot. There is surprise in her voice, but no criticism; it is simply an interested observation.

"That's just about where I saw it too," I say. "Now keep paying attention to where it goes each time and tell me if it is higher, lower, or in the same position as the one before."

I throw five more balls.

"A bit lower . . . higher . . . lower . . . the same . . . lower," Mary reports with objective interest. "They seem to be getting lower." I hear the same characteristic tone of surprise in her voice which tells me that she's not trying to take her racket anywhere, but just watching it happen. She seems to be genuinely curious about what the racket head will do next.

"Keep watching it," I say as I throw ten more balls.

"Still lower . . . the same . . . a little higher . . . lower . . . lower . . . the same . . . the same . . . the same . . . I think I have it now," she declares as her last ball, hit solidly, skims the net cord. "My racket is now at the same level as the ball. It feels much better. That's right, isn't it?"

Mary's stroke now looks more consistent. Most of the erratic elements have disappeared, and her backswing on the last three shots was close to waist-high. "Just keep in touch with your racket," is all I say.

Mary hits three more balls, but now her stroke suddenly looks more tight and deliberate. "Are you trying to take your racket back at waist level?" I ask.

"Well, sort of," she replies. "It began coming down of its own accord, but then it felt so much better and sounded so solid that the last few times I tried to repeat it."

"But what I'm curious about is what your racket will do if you neither try to correct what seems wrong nor try to repeat what is right. I want us to establish where your swing will end up if we just let it decide for itself." I throw several more balls and can see the curiosity returning to her face. The first stroke is waist-high, the second quite a bit higher, and the third slightly below the waist. Five of the next six balls are hit with slight topspin, and Mary's racket is finishing its swing at shoulder level, extended in front of her close to the classic ending of the follow-through. After ten more balls there is an effortless consistency in Mary's stroke. Balls are clearing the net by two to three feet. The backswing is no longer erratic but is repeatedly being taken back in a slightly circular motion to a spot about six inches below the waist before swinging forward and upward toward the ball.

"Where is your racket most of the time now?" I ask.

"Much lower," says Mary with surprise and interest. "It seems to have settled down just a bit below my waist."

"Does that seem okay to you?" I ask.

"I don't know if it's right or wrong, but it sure feels pretty good, and all of the balls are going over the net. I like it."

"Pretty smart racket you have there. Who taught it to swing like that?" Mary gets the point; there has been a lot of learning going on, but not much teaching.

"I guess I learned by myself, but it seems too easy."

"Yes, it's easy when you don't try to control it. But is it *too* easy?" Mary doesn't answer.

Before shifting Mary's attention away from the level of her racket, I return to "bounce-hit" for ten more balls to see whether her stroke will maintain its consistency when her mind is again focused on the ball. Not only does the level remaining consistent, but important developments have occurred in her follow-through, the angle of her racket, and her footwork. These changes have taken place peripherally and simultaneously with the change in her backswing.

There were three major phases in the above Inner Game

lesson. The first could be called "getting in touch with what is." This meant helping Mary to directly experience her racket so that she could feel it at any given moment. The second phase could be called "observing changes." Mary watched her swing changing stroke by stroke without consciously influencing it, until it stopped changing. The third phase was "grooving," allowing the new stroke to repeat itself until it occurs automatically, even when no attention is paid to it.

The next step is to focus Mary's attention on timing. "Mary, can you tell me where your racket head is at the moment that the ball bounces on its way to you? Is it in front of you, partway back, all the way back, or coming toward the ball?"

By this time Mary is beginning to know better than to ask me where I think her racket should be, and starting to trust her body to show her. She reports the position of her racket every two or three balls. "About here," she says, showing a position about halfway through her backswing. "Now it's back farther . . . still farther." Within only a few balls, she has felt her way to a timing which is comfortable and effective for her; her racket is almost entirely back by the time the ball bounces. I do not wait until it goes back as early as I take mine back, because for every individual the right timing is slightly different. Mary is the authority about what is right for her body at this stage in her development.

It should be stressed that in one hour Mary has enormously increased the effectiveness of her stroke without having to *remember* anything. She has also proved to herself through experience that her body can be trusted to learn to play tennis. Now she can continue the natural learning process on her own, or with the help of a teacher who will assist in bringing to her attention the various other elements of her stroke, including follow-through and footwork. The fundamentals of forehand, backhand, volley, serve and overhead can each be learned in the same way. Perhaps unthinking observation of the strokes of the pro will assist the process, but most essential is her increasing awareness of her own body and racket as they go through the changes called learning.

By this method strokes are allowed to develop organically, each change taking place when it is ready. The results are more solid and less contrived. Strokes depend not on self-instruction, but on clear images implanted in the memory of the body's computer. Moreover, the process does not involve frustration; since there is no trying, there is no failure. The player is surprised and delighted by his own progress, a progress for which he does not tend to take ego-credit because Self 1 has had only a modest part to play. Perhaps most important of all, the student comes to trust himself because the authority for right and wrong has proved to be within himself. He learned by "listening" and paying attention to his own body. The teacher was not an external authority, but merely someone who helped put him in touch with his own internal authority.

The player's trust in himself grows as the process is allowed to continue and proves effective. This trust is the true basis of the confidence needed by beginners and advanced players alike. Self-confidence means trust in self. What part of our self is trustworthy? This is the search of the Inner Game player. Experience has repeatedly shown me that the wisdom of my body is more to be trusted than the part of my mind which is constantly chanting the rights and wrongs, the shoulds and shouldn'ts. As these experiences continue, my trust of Self 2 increases and my reliance on Self 1 decreases.

Stroke Development for the More Advanced Player. This is basically no different from that for the beginner. Both progress by virtue of increased awareness. Once Toney, one of the women pros playing for World Team Tennis, asked me to spend some time with her on her serve. She brought a friend with her, and as we warmed up I was amazed to discover how stroke-conscious both girls were. They remarked on eight or ten little idiosyncrasies of my strokes as if searching for some new tip to help their own. I had assumed that by the time a player earned money from her tennis she had stopped thinking about it so analytically, but as I should have suspected, the opposite was true.

When it came time to look at Toney's serve, I could see a rather obvious hitch at the back of her motion which interfered with the fluidity of her swing and blocked a great deal of power otherwise available. Toney was eager to know what I was observing, but before she could question me I asked her, "What are *you* noticing?" She answered by providing an astoundingly complicated analysis of what was wrong with her serve. There were also two or three technical points that her team captain had been "working on" with her.

"Can you describe to me what this hitch is actually like? Can you swing in slow motion without tossing the ball up and show me how you *do* it?" But without hitting the ball, Toney couldn't really show me her hitch. "So how do you know that it's really there?" I asked.

"Well, I've seen it on video tape, and I've been told by a lot of coaches that it's there."

"Yes, but maybe it's gone away. Can you *feel* it now?"

"I don't know. But I do know that my serve hasn't been getting any better."

Toney served a few balls and there was a little less hitch. "Hey, that feels better. I think it's gone."

"I can still see it. Why don't you try to feel what shape and form this hitch has and exactly when it happens instead of simply deducing whether it's there by the results?"

Toney swung again. "Oh, that's awful!" she exclaimed. "There's a big ol' hesitation there. I never knew it was that bad. That's awful!"

"Pretend that there's nothing awful about it right now and simply try to tell me just when the hesitation starts and how long it lasts."

As Toney started to measure the length of hesitation with interest rather than condemnation, the pause decreased gradually, until there was a fluid motion. At first her rhythm and timing were thrown off, but soon she was tossing the ball up lower in order to make up for the shorter elapsed time of her swing. As fluidity and timing came together, Toney's power unlocked, and the change in the serve after only ten minutes was amazing.

"Thank you," she exclaimed. "I've been working on this for months without success. I just want to make sure that I don't forget what you told me."

"What did I tell you? I said nothing that you have to try to remember. The learning occurred when you experienced what you thought was that 'awful hitch' in your stroke. When you saw it just as it was, when you actually *felt* it happening, the learning began. Awareness of the difference was what gave you control. Therefore, when anything seems to be going wrong with your game, why not try increasing your awareness of how it *is* before slaving so hard on changing it?"

"Will that work?" she asked. There was anxiety in her voice, and I realized how much there is at stake for a player whose career depends on how she swings her racket. I can imagine that it takes more courage for a playing professional to let go of the traditional concepts of learning.

"Try and see" was all I could say, knowing that nothing but the evidence of her own experience would really convince her of the trustworthiness of the intelligence of her own body. But the overwhelming evidence of my own experience is that strokes correct themselves if you let them.

The Difficulty of Believing that Awareness Cures

One of the most difficult concepts for the player of the Inner Game to absorb is that awareness alone is enough to bring about needed changes in one's strokes—or in behavior in general. But day after day it happens before my eyes with student after student. Even so, I'm still surprised by it, because for years I, too, was conditioned to believe that improvement is a result of telling oneself what is wrong and what is right, and then trying hard to stop the one and do the other. If such a belief is strong enough, it sometimes makes it impossible for us to see or to admit that natural learning is taking place, even when we have directly experienced it. Players who observe that they have improved without instructions and without trying think there must be a gimmick, and want to be given some kind of tip which will ensure that the same magic happens next time. Often they attribute their improvement to me, and say it happens only when I'm around. But the fact is that it happens whenever *awareness* is around, provided that there is little interference from concepts and the imprecations of Self 1. But evidence mounts with each experience, and finally it becomes convincing: *Trying fails; awareness cures.*

To ease the sense of disbelief in the face of this evidence, I began wondering, *How* does awareness cure? I doubt if anyone thoroughly understands the process, but all that is required is an explanation that will remove the process from the realm of the magic.

Consider the following example. Suppose that you are playing tennis at dusk and that because of the limited light the visibility of the ball is reduced to 10 percent—not an uncommon experience for tennis addicts in the days before lighted courts. Suppose further that you are playing under the influence of a general anesthetic which cuts down the feeling of your body to only 10 percent. Under these conditions it is extremely difficult for you to know where your racket or the ball is. You see a round shadow approaching you, but it is difficult to perceive how fast it is coming or where it will land. You run toward the spot where you imagine the ball will bounce, but you are off balance and run too close to the ball. You couldn't tell that you were off balance until you were about to fall, nor that you were getting too close to the ball until you were already there. Because there was so little feedback from both the ball and your body, there was no way you could correct your imbalance or positioning until it was too late. Obviously, trying to play tennis under these circumstances would be frustrating. The body does, in fact, respond to feedback from the ball and the body in order to make even the smallest movement in tennis. We cannot operate without this feedback, and if it is limited the quality of our play will suffer accordingly.

On the other hand, if the feedback is increased—that is, if we become *more* aware—it stands to reason that the body's ability to correct itself will increase proportionately. In the preceding pages we have begun to see some of the handicaps we impose on ourselves which decrease awareness and therefore the quality of feedback. Easy examples are anxiety, thinking, trying, distractions. These mental activities produce a kind of dusk to hamper our play. When these interferences are removed or controlled, the light becomes brighter, the visual and kinesthetic feedback is amplified and becomes vivid in subtle detail. The slightest imbalance, overtightness or mispositioning of the racket registers in the body's computer (not in the thinking mind) while there is plenty of time for correction. This is analogous to a missile tracking a plane perfectly, the corrections taking place automatically and responding to the slightest changes in the target.

Letting Go of Overtightness

I believe that the greatest physical cause of error in tennis —and perhaps in any sport—is the tightening of too many muscles. The resulting rigidity prevents power, causes imbalance, jerks the racket out of its intended path and prevents the full release of energy in any body movement. Take a look at people as they hit tennis balls. You will see tension in their faces, shoulders, forearms, wrists and legs. With beginners who are full of self-doubt the tightness will be more pronounced, but many players advance to intermediate levels carrying their tension with them in every stroke, assuming unconsciously that it is an integral part of their power and control. Even the most advanced players make errors by tensing the wrong muscles at the wrong time. Most of our efforts to control our bodies are made by tightening our muscles, and since most of us are trying to control our bodies in one way or another for most of the period we are awake, we are too tense most of the time.

Overtrying is usually expressed in terms of overtightness. This observation is hardly a new one; perhaps the second most common instruction given by tennis pros to their students ("Watch the ball" being the first) is "Relax." But though telling oneself to relax seems a step in the right direction, it is really a very inexact method of releasing tension. When they first begin to relax a little, most players feel and actually play better, but it soon becomes difficult to know just how much to relax. Total relaxation would be literally to lie down on the court. To take a less extreme example, relaxing one's wrist at the moment of impact while volleying would deprive your shot of power and accuracy. Here we return to the point that every muscle movement is accomplished by the contraction of some muscles and the relaxation of others. The vague instruction to "relax" is wholly inadequate for the complex series of tightening and loosening of muscles necessary to complete any action in tennis. Only Self 2 is sophisticated enough to give the hundreds of muscles in your body the instructions necessary. In fact, sometimes when my Self 1 is getting a little arrogant and is thinking it knows how to play tennis, I suggest that if it really wants to run the show, it should learn the names of all the different muscles in the body, and which ones should be tight and which ones loose, moment by moment, for all the possible shots in tennis. Then it can work out a system of communication which will relay all the necessary instructions to these muscles in the split second allowed between perception and response. Faced with this, Self 1 becomes a little more humble, recognizes the superior intelligence and competence of Self 2 and places trust in it again.

But what can be done on a practical level to get rid of unnecessary tightness in one's stroke without becoming too loose?

Here is a method which helped Sandra, a conscientious and determined intermediate player who came for an Inner Game lesson. She had played for only two years, but already was wearing straps around one elbow and knee. After hitting only a few shots to her, I observed that she was very tense and was in the habit of judging each shot she made. When I asked her what she wanted to gain from our hour, she told me that she was doing a number of things wrong with her forehand and hoped she could correct them by the end of the lesson.

I took some time to explain to Sandra that the approach I would take in helping her forehand would involve neither analyzing what she was doing wrong nor suggesting corrections, but becoming more familiar with the way she was swinging now.

"As I hit these next balls to you, I simply want you to be aware of your body while you hit them. Don't think about correcting your forehand; just pay attention to how your body feels."

After a few balls I asked, "Did you feel any one part of your body more than another?"

Sandra put her left arm on her right forearm and replied, "I think I'm getting too close to the ball."

"You're touching your right forearm," I observed. "What did you feel there?"

"Oh, my arm felt kind of scrunched up," she answered.

"Scrunched up? Does it feel scrunched up right now?"

"No, just while I was hitting the ball."

"I'll hit you some more balls. See if you can tell me exactly *when* during the stroke you feel this 'scrunch,' okay?"

After a few balls Sandra said, "I feel it just as I begin to come forward to hit the ball, but to tell you the truth it wasn't as noticeable the last few times."

"What *did* you feel?" I asked.

"Well, my arm felt kind of tight."

"At what point?"

"I don't know. Let me see."

Sandra was becoming curious and less achievement-oriented. Before hitting her the next ball I asked, "Is there any tightness in your arm right now, *before* I hit the ball?"

"No," she reported. I waited an instant and could see her ready position relax a little.

After several more balls Sandra said, "There seems to be a little tightness as soon as I see the ball coming toward me, and then much more as I try to hit it. I know I should relax more. A lot of people have told me that, including my husband. They all say I'm too tight, but I can't seem to help it. I guess I just try too hard."

One of the most frustrating of criticisms is to be told that you try too hard. Soon you realize that you are trying hard *not* to try hard and are caught in a vicious circle. "I'm interested in this tightness," I replied. "Just how tense is your arm on these forehands? I want you to pay attention to the tightness in your arm on each of the next few balls and then measure it. Let's say that the degree of tightness on your last forehand measured three on a scale of zero to five. After each of the next forehands, call out the level of tightness you experience in your arm. If there's more, say four or five; if less, zero, one, or two."

As I hit the balls to Sandra she called after every shot: "Three . . . four . . . three . . . two . . . one . . . three . . . one . . . one . . . one . . . one . . . one." By now she was stroking much more freely and there was a detached but contented smile on her face.

"How do you feel?" I asked.

"Wow! I feel much more relaxed. That's amazing."

"Surprised?"

"Yes, because I'm not trying to relax. The tightness just went away. Mostly I'm surprised at how easy it seems to hit the ball. How did it happen?"

"Does it seem that your shots have more or less power?"

"I wasn't really paying attention, but it seems like more, or at least as much, but I'm using only half the effort."

As Sandra observed her forearm with new interest, muscles in the rest of her body began relaxing as well. Not all of them, however, and the process continued. As she listened to her body she became an increasingly discriminating observer of a process which led her toward the perfect balance for *her,* a balance she never could have attained if she had simply been told to relax.

This method of increasing body awareness is simple and broad in its application. The Inner Game teacher merely helps increase the awareness of that part of the body which comes naturally to the student's attention. He is asked exactly what is happening to the spot in question, and at what instant; that is, he is asked to catch the problem in the act and to measure its degree on repeated shots. By becoming aware of small increments of difference in feeling and in results, changes start taking place—and they stop only when the body has found what feels good for it and what works.

The beauty of this method is that the instructor never imposes his own concepts on another individual. The student's Self 2 picks the particular part of his body which needs attention, and the instructor then simply encourages increased awareness of this area until Self 2 has made the changes it is ready to accept at its present level of development. With this method there need be no common understanding between pro and pupil about what measure of tightness is ultimately desirable. Neither of them needs to form a judgment that, say, a "1" level is the best. Both merely observe the body without interference and wait to discover at what level it will choose to remain for this particular student. The results speak for themselves. This method is useful in facilitating change in any stroke at any level of competence.

Coping with Pain

A similar process can be employed in dealing with pain. Many players complain of pain caused by different strokes in different parts of their bodies, and nowadays an increasing number of straps and bandages appear on their arms and legs. Normally the player's reaction to pain is to try to ignore it: Don't think about it and maybe it will go away. Sometimes it does, but often the pain is caused by the way they hit the ball. By ignoring it, the cause continues and the injury gets worse.

The other common reaction to pain is to try to compensate for it. We ask ourselves what we are doing wrong and then try to correct it. But most pain in tennis is a result of trying too hard in the first place. Doing something different may seem to help at first, but in the long run it usually leads to exchanging one pain for another.

The Inner Game approach to pain in tennis is to increase one's awareness of it. If one experiences pain in a certain part of the body, I suggest neither ignoring nor attempting to correct for it. Place your attention on the part of the body experiencing the pain and locate it exactly. Determine what kind of pain it is—strain, tension, ache or sharp, biting twinge—and notice exactly when it occurs. Does it hurt even before you swing? Does its intensity increase at any particular part of your swing? As you localize when and where the pain is occurring, resist the temptation to analyze what you may be doing wrong. Leave that job to Self 2. When you have located the where and when, begin to discriminate the degree of hurt on succeeding shots by grading the level of pain on a scale of 1 to 10. This will absorb your attention. Don't try to avoid the pain or correct for it; simply experience it and observe objectively whether it increases or decreases with each swing. In this way your body will receive a very clear message as to which swings cause more pain and which less. Since the body doesn't enjoy hurting, it will select those which produce the least pain, yet are still effective.

During this process you will sometimes notice that your stroke or grip has altered, and will realize what changes your body is making to avoid the pain. But the point is not to conclude that this change has corrected what you've been doing wrong. Nor is there any need to remember it; the body won't forget. I have seen players take off straps from arms or legs after only a few minutes of this awareness drill and never wear them again.

It is important to remember, however, that the awareness drill cannot be expected to solve every problem. You should be careful to listen to your body objectively; if the pain doesn't lessen or disappear even after you have focused your awareness on its location, timing and intensity, it is probably because of an injury you have incurred during play rather than because of a fault in your swing. Then Self 2's message is clear: Don't swing a racket again until the injury heals.

I have seen people swing so contortedly when they serve that there is no way for them to avoid hurting themselves with every swing, but they are so intent on getting the ball in that they don't even *feel* the pain—until a couple of years later when they say, "Yesterday I served and ruined my elbow. I must have really done something wrong; my doctor said I shouldn't play again for a month." When you ignore the subtle messages of your body, Self 2 will find more obvious ways to catch your attention.

Here are some of the questions I might ask a student who complains of pain while serving:

Q. In what part of your body do you feel the pain?
A. Mostly in my elbow.
Q. Is it a dull ache or a sharp, biting pain?
A. It's more like a sharp, stabbing pain.
Q. Does it hurt right now?
A. No, only when I serve.
Q. There's no pain at all when you're not serving? Does your other elbow feel exactly the same right now?
A. Well, I can feel a little residual pain in my right elbow from the serving I've done so far, but only a little.
Q. Okay. Now I want you to serve again and notice at exactly what point in your serve the intensity of the pain is at its maximum. (Often this perception takes some time to arrive at because the instant of greatest pain is usually

at that point when the player is involved in trying to make contact with the ball, trying to put power into it, or trying to do something "right." It is often necessary to remind the student that the point of the exercise is not to improve his serve, but to learn something about the pain in his arm. It's easy to remember the pain, but to catch it exactly when it is occurring requires keeping your attention on your elbow every moment during the serve. When true awareness comes, it is usually reported with some surprise.)

A. Oh, I think the pain actually begins just after my racket starts toward the ball. Right here.

Q. Fine. Now, keeping your attention on your elbow, measure the intensity of the pain on each of the next few serves. Let's arbitrarily call your next serve five; then measure each of the next serves on a scale of zero to ten.

As you might expect, the changes that occur not only lessen the pain, but increase the effectiveness of the serve, for the motions which produce pain are almost always unnatural, inefficient ones.

Abandoning Caution and Increasing Power

Elaine, the conscientious wife of a doctor, had been taking Inner Game lessons for several months. At the beginning of each lesson her strokes were tight, but with a little coaxing she would relax, begin to enjoy herself and play better. Small but strong, she never was satisfied with the power of her serve. I had done awareness exercises with her before, so she had come to realize that most of the power in serving comes from the snap of the wrist; still, she had never really permitted herself to let go and allow her body to serve with the power I knew it was capable of. Instead she would always try to produce power by trying to force her shoulder; the arm would tighten and the result would be a restricted motion.

"I still don't seem to have any power on my serve," Elaine said one day.

"How much would you like?" I said, not knowing quite why I had asked the question.

"Lots," she answered with more emphasis than usual.

"Well, let's forget about all the power that *isn't* in your serve, and pay attention to what *is* there. After all, your serve does go over the net, which requires *some* power."

When Elaine started serving, I could see her right arm stiffening as she took her racket back. She pulled it down as if gravity didn't exist, then brought it up over her head. The elbow was too tight to bend much, so she hit the ball with her arm only half-cocked. I also noticed a characteristic tightness of the wrist. It looked as if her arm and racket were a right-angled lever being propelled by the shoulder muscle.

"Tell me, where do you think your power is coming from?" I asked.

I expected Elaine to answer that it came from her shoulder. She didn't answer for a few serves, then asked tentatively, "Could it be that my power is coming from my stomach?"

This remark didn't exactly fit my concept of what produces power in the serve. On the other hand, I knew from my experiences with yoga that the center of the body's power does in fact lie at a point just below the stomach called the *ki.* "Perhaps," I said. "Can you feel how the power gets from your stomach to the ball?"

Elaine served a few more times, describing what she was experiencing after each one. All the while her serve was picking up power.

"Yes, it comes up from my stomach, through my arm and out into the ball." Her arm seemed a bit more relaxed, but still had a way to go.

"How much power do you want to let out?" I asked.

"A lot," she said again. I could tell that she was still only partially letting go and was still trying to push the power out. Her shoulders and back remained tight and lurched forward toward the ball.

"How much of the total power that you have would you say you are actually letting out?"

"Oh, I suppose about fifty percent."

"So you're still hanging on to fifty percent?"

"Yeah."

"Okay, taking your last serve arbitrarily to represent fifty percent power and fifty percent in reserve, I want you to measure and report the extent to which you really let go on each serve."

Elaine reported as follows: "Sixty . . . forty . . . thirty . . . forty . . . sixty . . . seventy . . . fifty . . . seventy-five . . . seventy-five . . . seventy-five . . . seventy-five . . . seventy-five."

"Why not let go all the way next time and see what happens?"

"Seventy-five percent . . . seventy-five percent . . ."

"What's holding you back? Where are you doing it?"

"My stomach!" Elaine exclaimed in surprise. "I tighten my stomach."

I was surprised too. "Now serve again."

Crack! "That's the first time I've ever heard one of my serves *crack.*" Elaine was stunned; her serve had almost doubled in speed. She rushed to serve again, but this time she tried to regain the power, and of course lost it. "Wow, I really felt it just then! My stomach tightened just as I was about to hit the ball."

"You've been choking off your own power right at its source," I observed.

Crack! Crack! Crack! "It's a little scary, but I like it," she said. There was a self-possessed smile on her face I'd never seen before.

Often our power is inhibited by our attempt to gain power. Elaine tightened her stomach in order to push the power out, and as a result tightened her whole upper body. Likewise, trying to snap your wrist hard almost always results in tightening too many of its muscles and constricting the snap. We try hard to gain power when we doubt that we have enough already within us, and the effort itself in fact prevents us from achieving our aim. Self 1 is always complaining about the power that isn't there and trying to make up for it; Self 2 knows the power that *is* there and how to release it. The way to release power is not to try to add it, but to cut the strings that are keeping it locked inside. Power comes from letting go, not tightening up, from an awareness of what *is* there rather than a compensation for what's *not.*

Grace, Balance, Rhythm and Footwork

As with power, there is one key to increasing your balance, rhythm or footwork—what might be called the *poise* in your game. The secret is to increase your awareness of the desired quality. Most players complain that they are all too aware of a *lack* of balance, a *lack* of rhythm, a lack of proper footwork. They say they feel awkward and uncoordinated, but in the process of trying to overcome these flaws they inevitably become more awkward.

Hence, when David, one of my students, complained that his game "lacked grace" and that he felt awkward when he moved, it would not have done any good if I'd tried to help him gain grace. Rather, my job was to help him experience the grace that was already within him, no matter how hidden it was.

David was an intellectual and a psychotherapist, and from early childhood had been conditioned to think that he was smart but not athletic. Now he wanted to achieve some standard of excellence in a sport, but because of a deeply ingrained belief in his own awkwardness he could not seem to move to the ball efficiently. On the court he always looked as if he was trying desperately to overcome his apparent lack of coordination—and in the process looked very uncoordinated.

I would ask David how he felt when he ran toward the ball, and he would always answer, "Awkward as hell!"

Since he enjoyed analyzing a problem, I once asked him, "Just what do you mean by 'awkwardness'? What are you actually aware of?"

"I feel a distinct lack of balance and rhythm, and my legs don't ever seem to be where I'd like them to be. I feel clumsy all over."

"Could it be that you are aware of *some* grace, but just not quite as much as you would like? Could you even know that you were awkward if you hadn't experienced at least a little grace? I'm going to hit you some running backhands and forehands and ask you to tell me if you can sense any more grace and balance on one side than you can on the other."

I hit David five shots to either side.

"There seems to be considerably more grace on my forehand," he reported afterwards.

"How can you tell?"

"It's hard to describe; it simply feels easier and more natural. I can feel the difference in both my legs and my arms."

"Okay, let's focus on those sensations of easiness and naturalness. Do you like them?" I hit him several more forehands and he returned them with a little more ease.

"Now let your legs do whatever they want. Don't force them into the proper position; let them be clumsy if they want to be. Just let go of all control and let them do what they like."

This time there was a significant change in the way David moved. "My legs don't seem to want to be as awkward as I thought they would; in fact, there's a lot more grace than before. That's amazing. Maybe I'm not so uncoordinated as I thought. Let's see what I can do with my backhand."

We went through about the same process on the other side, and within a few moments the so-called lack of coordination dissolved before our eyes. It was beautiful. "I'm playing better than I feel I deserve," said David analytically, and then added with surprise, "But I guess that's what grace is all about."

"That's what the whole Inner Game is about: allowing ourselves to play better than we feel we deserve. We can either hate our lack of grace, or love the grace we do have, no matter how small it may seem. Of these two different ways of looking at life, which do you think works best?"

It was only after this lesson with David that I realized that when I think I feel, say, my serve growing weaker, what I am really experiencing is less *strength*. However, I still have *some* strength left. There really is no such thing as *weakness*; there is simply more or less power. By thinking that I am weak or clumsy, I become enmeshed in an illusion and waste energy trying to compensate for something that in reality isn't there.

Summary

The principle of body awareness is simple. If you want to make something change, you must become more aware of the quality *as it now is*. If you want to improve a certain function of your body, don't be in too great a hurry to try to change it; first make the effort to observe it as it works here and now. In this way you will cooperate with the natural learning process and will achieve two results: (1) those elements of the function that were not effective for *your* purposes will tend to dissolve; (2) those elements that *were* effective will be reinforced.

The simple body-awareness procedures described in this chapter can be applied to every part of you, every movement and every stroke. In stroke development it is important to become more knowledgeable about the entire path of your racket on every stroke. You should become so sensitive to your racket that you come to experience it as an integral part of your body, so that whenever it leaves one of its grooved swings you will instantly be aware of it. Search your body for overtightness and pain. Focusing on these will encourage spontaneous changes that will not only dispel the tension from your tennis but increase your confidence in your body's ability to self-correct. Finally, you can increase awareness of your body's balance, rhythm, grace and power step by step. As you experience more of these qualities as they now are, they will become evident in your play. It may sound paradoxical, but it works.

The preceding chapters have elaborated on the basic Inner Game cycle introduced in Chapter 2. The distortions in the way we perceive a ball affect the way we respond to it; in turn, this affects our self-image, which again leads to distortion in perception. Chapters 2 and 3 discussed how to break out of this circle at the level of perception by attempting to dispel the distortions we project on the ball so that we can perceive it as it really is. The last two chapters have emphasized breaking the circle at the level of response by introducing methods for reducing tightness, pain and awkwardness in the body, and increasing racket and body awareness. The subject of the next chapter is how to help you break free of the limitations of self-image.

6
Self-Image

I know of no single factor that more greatly affects our ability to learn and perform than the image we have of ourselves. Who we think we are influences everything we do, every thought we have, every feeling we allow. The most dramatic and most lasting changes that take place in people's tennis —or in their life—occur when they abandon a concept of self which had previously limited their performance.

When Arthur Ashe at the age of thirty-one overcame the mental barrier which prevented him from believing that he could ever be more than a "good" player, he became the champion he had never before let himself be. Instead of playing his best once in a while, he began to play his best most of the time, winning almost all of the major tournaments in which he played. His game improved dramatically at a time when he was well past his physical prime. (Note: Since breaking through to greatness, Ashe has had another struggle with sustaining this image. "I can tell you one thing —" he told a reporter after losing early in the 1976 Wimbledon championship, "having everyone expect you to be the champion is not at all relaxing.")

Whenever a person attains a new, more realistic understanding of who he is, a quantum jump occurs in his ability to perform, whether in sport, business, or personal relations. He is able to express a new dimension of himself that he has literally grown to understand.

Self-Judgment and the Forming of a Negative Self-Image

Few players are aware of how they form the negative self-images which distort their perceptions and hamper their tennis. The first step to lessening these inhibiting effects of self-image is to perceive how they are formed and then to catch them in the act. If you listen to the voice of Self 1, whether in your own head or coming out of your mouth, you will discover that one of its favorite activities is to define itself. It is constantly thinking, I am this but not that; I can do this but not that; I like this but not that. It consistently identifies itself with your performance, measures itself relative to others, and does its pathetic best to dispel ignorance about who you are.

The trouble is that the way Self 1 goes about building concepts and beliefs about your identity is usually not only distorted but cancerous. Let's step inside the mind of a tennis player called Joe and see how those distortions take place, how they grow and what their effect is. If his thoughts seem similar to any of those in your own mind, I'm sure that the resemblance is purely coincidental.

Warming up before his match, Joe mis-hits his first three backhands and says to himself, What terrible shots! He's beginning to wonder if his backhand will be on or off today. He tries to correct his stroke, but misses a couple more and thinks, My backhand really is lousy today. He may even say this out loud to let his opponent know that he's usually a lot better.

Two subtle but important things have happened between his first thought and second. First, the negative judgment moved from the ball, the "terrible shots," to *his* lousy backhand. The judgment moved closer to *himself* and defined one of his possessions, his backhand. Already Joe is suffering from two crippling distortions. There is nothing really good or bad about a ball or a shot, though certainly some don't go where we intend them to. If "bad" is simply a *description* of the event, it is harmless, but usually it is a moral judgment imposed by Self 1 and has no reality when applied to balls, shots or backhands. As Hamlet says to Rosencrantz and Guildenstern, "There is nothing either good or bad but thinking makes it so." The second Self 1 distortion is creating the expectation that, based on his performance during the warm-up, Joe's backhand will be off all day. After a few more backhand errors, Joe exclaims, "I can't hit a backhand to save my life!" "Can't" is one of the most loaded words employed in defining oneself and in limiting one's potential. The negative judgment has now moved from being one of Joe's possessions to the very core of his potential; in effect, he is saying that he lacks even the potential to hit a backhand. Notice also that the word "today" has been casually dropped, thereby extending the judgment indefinitely. If Joe were reading this passage, he would probably interject here that he really didn't mean what he'd said. Perhaps he didn't, but my experience is that when we allow these thoughts to voice themselves they have a tendency to fester. Soon we *do* mean them, and begin to perform as if they were true.

When the match starts, Joe misses a few easy forehands and begins to think of himself as a terrible tennis player. The cancer has grown and spread still farther. With the word "am" the judging has reached the heart of Joe's self-image. "Am" is the most powerful word we use to define our identities. Possessions can be changed, potential can perhaps develop, but our *amness* is pretty rigid; almost any word we put after the phrase "I am" limits our potential. Moreover, the judgment has spread horizontally, to include Joe's whole game. He hasn't even hit a volley yet, but already every stroke is off and he *is* a lousy tennis player.

Joe's game deteriorates still further, living up to the reputation of his self-created image, and soon he is telling himself, I'm an uncoordinated bastard. Now his negative self-identification includes all physical activities that he's ever played, as well as those he hasn't. Though he doesn't realize it at the moment, he's increasing his chances of breaking a glass while washing the dishes that evening.

Joe loses his match to a player he thought he really should have beaten, and goes home thinking that he's no good at anything. Now there are no limits at all to his negative judgment—which, you will recall, had no basis for existence in the first place. Depressed, he will proceed to act out this self-image at home, and his family will suffer because of a few missed tennis shots.

It would seem that this negative thought process could go no further, but it does. I was reminded of the last step one day when appearing on a television program. The interviewer, a woman, greeted me enthusiastically, saying, "Oh, I'm so glad to meet you; maybe you can help my game. You see, my backhand . . . well, it simply doesn't exist!" When that thought generalizes, it becomes the final self-condemnation: I don't exist, I'm a nothing.

With remarkably little practice Self 1 can go through the entire process from "What a lousy shot that was" to "I'm a nothing" within a few seconds, and has the power to make you behave as if these thoughts were really true. Such judgments are usually formed on the basis of limited experience of one's performance and then quickly broadened to identify one's whole self. Thus, self-image becomes a role we act out, often preventing us from really experiencing our true selves or expressing our potential.

Role Playing

In order to demonstrate the effect of self-image on performance, I often ask a student to experiment in role playing. For example, I might suggest to a beginner struggling with self-doubt that he pretend he is a touring professional. "Let's assume that we're filming a television show, and that you're an actor who's been cast in the role of a professional tennis player. As the director, I ask you to act supremely confident, even to the point of arrogance. Swing at every ball as if you'd been playing all your life and were giving a demonstration to an admiring audience. Let yourself show off. Don't worry about where the balls go or what your strokes look like because we'll dub them in the film and they'll all look terrific. All that's important is that you identify with the personality and expectations of a pro who's been playing all his life; let his confidence show on your face and in your manner. Act the part no matter where the balls actually go; remember that this pro never expects to miss a shot—and when he does, it's always someone else's fault."

It's amazing to see what can happen to the beginner's strokes and style immediately after assuming his new role. He forgets his tentativeness; the hesitations and jerkiness leave his swing and he starts stepping into the ball as if he fully expected to make a great shot. When he does hit in this way, he accepts it as a matter of course, and when he misses he looks surprised. He may not really fool bystanders into thinking he's a champion, but he will realize that the beginner's role he was playing previously was itself largely an act that prevented him from playing as well as he really could. Most of us are unaware of the ways we limit ourselves in all areas of our lives by the roles we play derived from our Self image. By perceiving the difference between our roles and who we really are, we can vastly extend the range of possibilities for ourselves.

Letting Go of Self-Image

What always amazes me is how quickly a self-image can be formed, how powerfully it can affect our performance on the court, and yet how quickly it can be thrown off, resulting in immediate and significant changes in one's play. A good example of this occurred one day in a lesson with Arnie which was given in the presence of ten teaching pros who were interested in learning more about the Inner Game process.

"What would you like to work on?" I asked Arnie, after he had volunteered to be a guinea pig.

"I don't know. I guess my volley is about the worst part of my game."

"Okay, let's take a look at it," I said, and began hitting him forehands and backhand volleys. His shots were jerky and tight, with a tentative, uncertain swing, and he hit most balls parallel to his body. He faced the net on most shots, mis-hit often, and shook his head in self-criticism and disappointment after almost every shot.

Looking at Arnie's stroke, I could see at least a dozen technical mistakes. After about twenty balls, during which time I had said nothing but had simply paid attention to both his stroke and his body language, which revealed much of what he was feeling, I approached him at the net. I didn't know exactly what to say. "You don't look too happy," I observed.

"No," he answered, "I can never seem to hit it the way I'd like to."

"How would you like to be able to hit it?"

"Well, I'd like to hit it more—"

"No, don't tell me in words—*show* me. Here, I'll hit you a couple and you demonstrate how you'd like to be able to hit the ball." Quickly I began hitting balls to him before he had time to think, and immediately he started hitting forceful, authoritative volleys. He was stepping into the ball, meeting it out in front and putting shots away.

"Is that what you meant? More like that?" I asked.

"Yes, I'd like to be more in command of the situation, but I'm always on the defensive."

"I see. Well, hit a few more so that I can get a clearer idea."

Much to the amazement of all the teaching pros, as well as myself, Arnie continued to hit crisp volleys off both sides. Most of his technical errors had completely disappeared. Only Arnie seemed generally unimpressed. "Yeah, that's more like the way I'd like to hit them, but . . ." He hesitated; he'd been about to say "but I don't know how" when he realized for the first time what had happened: he *was* hitting his volleys the way he wanted to. For a moment Self 1 had been tricked: Arnie had forgotten the role he had been playing of the man with a weak volley; he hadn't formed the belief that he couldn't show me how he would like to be able to hit the volley—that was for an entirely different proposition. In the process, he also showed himself, so now Self 1 had a problem: Am I someone who can hit authoritative volleys or not? "Well, I doubt if I can keep doing that," said Arnie, smiling sheepishly.

"Why not?" I asked, hitting him some more balls. Immediately Arnie went back to his old style. "Right, that's the old volley," I observed. "Now show me again the way you'd like to be able to it." Again the tentativeness and overtrying disappeared and Arnie punched four putaways. Then, recognizing that he was again hitting balls the way he'd thought he couldn't, he lapsed back into ten weak, awkward shots.

"Hit the ball in such a way that even if you miss it, it will still have been fun," I suggested. "Regardless of the result, swing the way you'd really like to." Back came the confident, unrestrained strokes.

The struggle was on between the old image and the new reality, and Arnie wavered between the two for a while. Finally I heard myself being uncharacteristically authoritative. "Dammit, Arnie, why don't you just leave that other crap and volley the way you really want to. You can, you know, so do it!"

And he did. The frown on Arnie's face turned into an almost sensual victorious smile and he began consistently hitting shot after shot the way he had always wanted to.

I admired Arnie's courage. Even afterwards he was a little shaken; he simply didn't know whether to believe his memory of the volleys he had just hit or the memory of all the prior volleys missed. "I find it hard to believe," he exclaimed. "I don't really know how I did it. I think I was moving my feet differently, wasn't I?" He was looking for some technical trick to latch on to in order to make sure that his improved volley would stay with him.

"A lot of things changed," I said. "Ask the pros here. Your footwork, your stroke, your facial expressions. But mainly what changed was that for a moment you forgot your concept of yourself as a bad volleyer. When that image vanished, you were able to free the volleyer you really are and always have been. You simply released the volley that was there all the time. There's probably still a bit more left in there waiting to come out. But if you doubt yourself and try to get rid of what remains of the old volley by *making* yourself do what is technically correct, you will still be stuck because that's the you that was hitting those tight, try-hard balls off the wood."

After the exercise I asked Arnie to speak for the self that had hit the initial volleys. He thought for a minute and then answered, "I don't have a very good volley. I'm unsure of myself. But I know how I *should* hit it. I can improve if I try hard to hit the ball right. I don't like the ball not going where I want it to." Speaking for the second volleyer, Arnie said, "I'm in charge around here. I don't care where the ball goes; I'm going to hit it the way I want to. I'm in command and my ball *will* go where I want it to!"

Clearly, the two Arnies weren't fully at peace in those fifteen minutes, but he did gain insight into the relationship between his performance and his self-image, and saw how the nature of the self-image could lock or unlock his potential.

Image Barriers

The most prevalent example of the effect of self-image on performance is the phenomenon I call "the three-ball person." This is the player who after returning the ball three times, thinks to himself, Wow, this is a long rally! and misses the next shot. It's remarkable how many players recognize this characteristic from their own experience and can tell you without hesitation whether they become nervous after three, four, five or six balls. They know their own barriers well.

This quirk is clearly not based on one's actual ability; it is no more difficult to hit the second three balls over the net than the first three. Nor does it follow the law of averages. A person with the ability to hit three balls back might be expected to also have within him a few six-ball rallies, perhaps even some nines, but that's not what happens. Within one or two shots after his self-imposed limit, the player will miss. The three-baller is excited on attaining his norm, anxious after the fourth, and so panicky after the fifth that he never sees a six-ball rally.

Actually, the same phenomenon also occurs with advanced players. If a first-rate player hits two great passing shots in a row, he's apt to be nervous about trying a third. If he serves two aces in a row, he can't quite believe it, tries hard to do it again and double-faults. Each individual's cracking point depends on the self-image he has accumulated from past experience and from what others expect of him. A good golfer might not panic after making two birdies in a row, but if he hits six straight he might. The point is that most of us find something frightening about surpassing our own or others' expectations, and this fear usually keeps us from doing it. We identify with these expectations, and don't like to rock the boat by exceeding them. The four-minute mile was an enormous image barrier in the minds of thousands of milers, but within a year of its being broken, many were able to run that fast.

Breaking the Image Barrier by Concentration

One of the easiest ways of breaking through the image barrier is to focus your attention so completely on something that you "forget" to be afraid as you are about to exceed your expected limit. When a player's mind becomes absorbed in "bounce-hit," "seeing the trajectory" or "riding the ball," it is not at all unusual for him to progress from a three-baller to a thirty-baller without experiencing any anxious thoughts as he passes way beyond his image barrier. If he is doing the drill properly, he stops projecting his negative expectations on the ball and consequently does not distort his swing. Self 1 is no longer involved in returning the ball, but simply in observing it as it is; it is concentrating, not playing, and consequently does not consider itself on trial. But often the fear will occur afterwards, when the player will say to himself, Wow, that was the longest rally I've ever had! I can't believe it. He is more apt to think that there's some kind of magic in "bounce-hit" than to realize that all along he has had the potential to return thirty balls. Such a recognition might be too great a shock to his self-image.

Likewise, an advanced player who begins to get nervous because he is close to upsetting a player he's "not supposed" to beat, can break through his own expectations of losing simply by focusing all his attention on one shot at a time. If he can become engrossed in the present, point by point, and forget about the future, there is no doubt he can upset his opponent. But if he lets his mind dwell on thoughts of victory and all the attendant consequences, he's apt to experience anxiety, an unconscious let-up and lapses in concentration, and as a result will lose the match just as expected.

The effectiveness of techniques of such concentration depends on the extent of the control the player has developed over his mind, as well as on the strength of the self-image at stake. If the particular concept of self is very strong because it has been built up over a long period of time and has become an integral part of the way one defines oneself, it will be extremely hard to break through the barrier without experiencing fear. Concentrating on the moment will help, but something more—perhaps an insight or a series of strong experiences—may be required to jolt the player out of his self-imposed rut.

Fear after Breaking the Image Barrier

One of the most common occurrences after an Inner Game lesson is the experience of fear by a student who has just made a dramatic improvement. I recall one session with Bob, an intermediate player who wanted badly to improve. We were doing an awareness drill called "targeting" because he felt that his ground strokes lacked accuracy. Bob became absorbed in the exercise, and at one point knocked over the three tennis-ball cans placed around the court with three successive balls. Since he had never before hit a single target, he could barely contain himself. "I can't believe it!" he exclaimed with a huge smile on his face, and then added, "That's the most frightening thing that's ever happened to me." When I asked him why, all he could say was "Well, I can't *do* that. *You* know I can't do it, don't you?"

Once a girl who had thought of herself as "uncoordinated" suddenly began running smoothly and athletically to the ball and consistently hitting it in the center of her racket. After twenty such shots she stopped abruptly and said, "I can't go on, I'm scared to death." She was taking her lesson in front of about fifty people and had been nervous before going out on the court because she felt that she looked so uncoordinated. But now she was shaking like a leaf, twice as frightened as before. Recognizing her fear, I gave her time to calm down by asking her what was so frightening, and she replied, "I really thought that I was uncoordinated, but now I'm afraid to believe that I'm not. I don't know what to believe."

What is this fear that we experience as we approach an image barrier, and what is the fear afterwards? Clearly it's a terror of changing one's self-image. Bob would be delighted to believe that he was more accurate than he had thought, just as the uncoordinated woman would like to believe that she was not, but both were reluctant to place their faith in present evidence rather than the weight of years of contrary experience. If they were to believe that they really had the potential to play at higher levels than previously attained, it would hurt all the more if they didn't achieve their new plateau. The uncoordinated woman didn't like being clumsy, but the fact that she didn't expect more of herself softened the blow. To dare to expect more of oneself entails risking the pain of not living up to higher expectations. Self 1 looks at it this way: it's great to be a winner—but only if you can be sure that you're going to keep it up. Otherwise, according to its point of view, it's preferable to remain at a level that can always be maintained. With such reasoning most people mire themselves in levels of mediocrity far below their potential.

Three of Self 1's Methods to Distort Self-Image

From the above examples, as well as from our own experience, we can see that Self 1 has an extraordinary ability to create self-delusions which bear very little resemblance to reality. In doing so, it can create its own reality, which masks our ability to know ourselves and express our true capabilities. We think that we can't hit a backhand; then, believing this, we miss one and say to ourselves, I was right; I can't hit a backhand. Self 1 has created a false reality, so that we think something isn't there which actually is.

A second way in which Self 1 distorts self-image is just the opposite of the above—that is, it thinks it can do things which it can't, or that it is something which it really isn't. For example, a woman with only an average voice may decide that she wants to be an opera star. By this unrealistic hope she is following her mind instead of discovering her true potential, and so she suffers accordingly.

A third method used by Self 1 to distort self-image is to correlate character with performance, especially on a limited basis—for example, concluding that because you play erratic tennis one day, you are erratic in the rest of your life. Let's take a closer look at each of these ways of distorting our self-image, and at some exercises for dispelling them.

An Example of Distortion No. 1, or Trying to Fill Holes That Don't Exist

People continually look at themselves and see what they aren't. For example, they see little power and conclude that they have none, little coordination and decide they are clumsy, little love and feel that there is none in their lives. As a result, their goals are directed toward finding these values outside themselves. In short, Self 1 likes to see the holes—holes which don't exist—and then try to fill them.

One day a college basketball coach who was attempting to apply Inner Game principles to his instruction asked me to lunch in order to discuss his team. Though my Self 1 felt the pressure of a deadline for completing the manuscript of this book, I accepted the invitation. We spoke about many subjects, but of one in particular: a new forward on his team whom he was trying to help. "Charlie is tall, coordinated, and has a lot of talent," the coach said, "but he just isn't aggressive under the boards. I'd noticed this lack, but wanted to handle it nonjudgmentally, so during a break in a scrimmage I called Charlie aside and asked him, 'Have you ever noticed that you aren't aggressive under the boards?' Charlie answered, 'Yeah, Coach, as a matter of fact, I have.' I said, 'Okay, I was just checking,' and walked off."

"Then what happened?" I asked.

"Well, Charlie played the next quarter like a tiger, and the next day he came down to my office to talk to me more about what I meant by being aggressive. Was this the right Inner Game approach?" asked the coach.

"There is no one 'right' approach," I answered, "but I imagine that your forward was surprised not to get a lecture on how to be more aggressive. It was probably a big relief to him. It sounds as if he then went out and really *tried* to be aggressive. But tell me honestly, was he really more effective under the boards than before?"

"Well, he didn't know exactly how to be aggressive effectively. He tried hard—maybe a little too hard. He fouled quite a bit and looked pretty awkward."

"Sort of like a tiger 'trying to be a tiger'?"

"Yeah."

"He didn't get any lecture from you on how to do it, so he had no choice but to be aggressive according to his own concept of aggressiveness. Then, because this didn't work so well and because he wanted to live up to your expectations, the next day he came to see you to find out more about your idea of aggressiveness in order to solve this defect. Perhaps another approach might work better. Actually, your forward had been showing *some* aggressiveness all along; there just wasn't enough of it to get the job done. So we could assume that the necessary aggressiveness is already there, but for some reason is not expressing itself. If this is the case, your job as coach would be to help your forward to discover his latent aggressiveness by observing the aggressiveness he already displays. The chances are that when he began to do this, he would discover more about the quality and would be able to let more of it out. For example, perhaps he's been afraid of his aggressiveness because he was always bigger than others, and so he submerged it and worked at developing his coordination and ball control instead. But if he can be helped to perceive the aggressiveness he *already* expresses on the court, he can easily learn to distinguish between those forms that are appropriate in the game and those that aren't. As a result he will then overcome the fear which was keeping his aggressiveness locked up, and will be able to express what is appropriate. He won't be trying to force himself to conform to any concept, yours or his own, about how aggressive he should be. His actions will develop more organically, more naturally and probably more effectively."

The principle behind this approach is that you can't teach aggressiveness or any other desired quality which you assume isn't there; all you can do is to encourage the expression and development of those qualities which already exist. At one point in my life, I realized that I was spending an inordinate amount of energy trying to fill up holes in my personality and character which in fact did not exist. School had taught me that I was stupid in the process of becoming smart; my church had convinced me that I was bad in the process of becoming good. The negative always defined my essence, and growth meant adding "desirable" qualities—that is, becoming something that I essentially wasn't. It took many years and a lot of suffering before I understood that in essence I was fine the way I was, and that in order to grow I had only to rid myself of the limitations which had trapped me into thinking and acting differently.

Expressing Qualities. One good awareness exercise that I have found helpful in overcoming the limitations of seeing holes that aren't there and trying to fill them up is called "expressing qualities," and is one of my favorite ways of playing the Inner Game. I pick a quality in which I believe I am lacking, one which I think doesn't usually manifest itself. Then I focus on it, however little of it there seems to be, and try to express it in my play. I might pick a quality like authority because I feel I don't usually hit with authority. But there's always some of it in me, and I let it express itself in every shot I make. As I express whatever is there, it usually begins to increase. The purpose of the drill is to let it all come out. Since one never knows quite what to expect, the results are almost always surprising. Playing this game greatly expands my possibilities on the court.

I have one caution about this game. It is all too easy to imagine how an authoritative player would behave on the court—hitting hard, being aggressive in tactics and so forth. But if I *imitate,* I am only *trying* to be authoritative, and of course this is the same old game I've played all my life: attempting to be something I'm afraid I'm not—trying to fill up the holes by adding a quality to myself. But to express one's *own* authority is something quite different; you simply focus on the authority already within you and let it all out. You're not *adding*; you're merely *subtracting* whatever has been keeping that quality imprisoned. It's a very different experience—rewarding and a lot of fun.

One further warning. After you start expressing yourself without any preconceived notion of what's going to happen, Self 1 will often attempt to create a concept out of what Self 2 has just expressed, and then to force you to maintain it. For instance, I may let my authority express itself in a couple of returns of serve. Self 1 notices that I'm hitting the ball much more in front of my body than usual, and that I'm not hesitating during my swing. From this it will devise the theory that authority is expressed by not hesitating and by meeting the ball out front, and that this is what you should try to keep doing. But if you fall for this, all spontaneity is lost. Once again you are doubting your own authority and trying to make it happen because you doubt that it will. Frustration is sure to follow soon. When this happens, let go of the concept and simply continue expressing what is there, just being yourself. Then the fun will return and so will the growth.

Distortion No. 2: Thinking You Are Something That You Aren't

This is another creative trick of Self 1. It starts telling you, for example, that you can be the greatest tennis player in the world, disregarding your actual talents. A million players can dream this, but only one of them can actually be the best. Twins may both decide they want to become doctors. One may have the true interest and latent potential and realize his goal; the other, who may be a potential artist, tries for the same career, thereby stunting his natural capabilities.

It took me a long while to realize that all I should expect of myself was the fulfillment of my own potentialities, and that it wasn't necessary to try to live up to the concepts that my Self 1 or others attempted to impose on me. I'm still learning that lesson, and every day experience more freedom as I learn a little more. Maybe the most important thing I have learned is that the development of any particular talent or quality that is part of my individual potential is not so important as fulfilling the potential I share with all human beings: to know, to respect, and to love life itself.

The Ghost in the Closet. Under the category of imagining what isn't there is "the ghost in the closet" syndrome. In this Self 1 hypothesizes that there is a monster inside itself which would do terrible things if allowed out—that is, *deep down there's something basically wrong with me.* Out of fear the individual avoids the monster or the closet in which he is supposedly hiding. Though the monster may never have manifested itself and in fact doesn't really exist, it has a great influence on the person's behavior. One day, looking for something to keep it busy, Self 1 may even get brave and decide to rid itself of this self-created ghost, so it hires an exorcist of sorts, there being many about, and promises to follow the instructions given. Sure enough, the exorcist does his magic and eventually tells Self 1 that the ghost isn't there, or even that he can enter the closet now because it's safe. In one sense the exorcist hasn't accomplished anything by ridding Self 1 of something that wasn't there in the first place, but for the person who has imagined the monster's existence and whose behavior has been influenced, everything seems different. Self 1 has only created and destroyed its own illusion, leaving the reality beneath unaltered, though perhaps more apparent.

There are two basic ways I know of to deal with ghosts. One is to accept their apparent reality and respond to them on their own level. My father helped me get rid of nightmares about wolves by telling me that wolves hated to be punched in the nose. The next time I dreamed about a wolf, it was chasing me and I was running as fast as I could. Finally I got into the family car, but one window was open and the wolf leaped up as I was hurriedly closing it. But only his snout made it through the space at the top, and of course I popped him on the nose as hard as I could. The wolf ran off howling and those nightmares never bothered me again.

The other way to deal with wolves that aren't there is to stop creating them—that is, wake yourself up and realize that they are simply your own creations, and that you have complete control over them.

Breaking the Image Illusion by the Power of Acceptance.
Often I've found that an essential step in freeing yourself from the limitations of your self-image is acceptance of yourself as you *appear* to be—even if this, too, is simply an illusion.

Ted, whose father had been a teaching professional, had a problem with his forehand for more than twenty years. He had been a good player in high school, but during college he had lost confidence in his game, especially in his forehand. "It got so bad that I virtually gave up the game," he told me.

"Now I play only once or twice a year just to see if the problem is still there."

I asked Ted if he would be willing to work on his forehand during a workshop I was giving in Denver, and he agreed. "I'd really like to believe that something could help me. I know my problem is totally mental; I just don't have any confidence," he said.

It was clear to me that what Ted labeled a lack was actually more a ghost which seemed to materially affect his performance. I decided to try an awareness exercise so that we'd have a clearer picture of what was happening. I started by hitting Ted backhands, which he returned firmly and with underspin. There was a little overtrying, but basically it was a sound and reliable shot. However, his first few forehands revealed a different story. There was a huge hitch in his stroke between the time the racket began to come forward and actual contact. He took the racket back high, but on the way down his wrist would turn to spaghetti for a split second and the ball would spin sideways off the open face of his racket. There was little power and almost no control. Ted's face was tight and expressionless, and it was clear that the entire experience was unpleasant for him.

I asked Ted to hit as many forehands as he liked and to focus as much as he could on what was happening. After five or six shots I asked him what he had experienced.

"I don't think I'm stepping into the ball enough."

Actually, he was, though stiffly. "Anything else?" I asked, wondering what he would say about the obvious hitch in his swing.

"No, not really," Ted answered, "just a total lack of confidence." The ghost was alive and well, but as yet unseen.

"Fine," I said. "But what are you aware of in your body —your swing, for instance."

"Nothing, really."

The fifty people who were watching were as amazed as I was that Ted was unaware of the huge hitch in his swing. "I'm going to hit you some more forehands," I said, "and I want you to pay close attention to your arm. Tell me as much as you can about what happens on the backswing and the foreswing."

After ten balls I asked Ted for a report, and he replied, "Really, all that I'm aware of is a big lapse in confidence whenever I swing on the forehand side." He was so locked into his concept that he couldn't feel his body.

"Take a practice swing without the ball exactly the way you swing when it is coming," I suggested. Ted's stroke was totally different, without a hitch. "Is that the way you swing?" I asked.

"Yes, I think so." Clearly something in Ted was refusing to be aware of that hitch. It was as if he blanked out from the time he took the racket back until he hit the ball. Yet it was so obvious to the viewers that they couldn't have been more surprised if he'd said that he didn't know he was on a tennis court.

For the next five minutes I worked with Ted on allowing himself to swing without any confidence while I maintained a steady stream of talk. "Okay, go ahead and swing without confidence. Show me how you hit your forehand when you've lost all your confidence." This was my way of accepting the ghost. I even congratulated him when the hitch became bigger, and feigned criticism when it shrank. Finally Ted was able to feel the hitch and to accept its presence. I told him to make no effort to get rid of it, but to get to know it exactly as it was. The moment he felt it strongly enough to be truly aware of it, it began to disappear and he started hitting strong topspin forehands with a loop swing in a radically different stroke pattern and style. At first the balls flew out, but soon most of them, brought down by the topspin, were diving deep into the court. The onlookers were gasping, trying to hold back their congratulations for fear of making Ted self-conscious.

Finally I stopped and asked how these new shots had felt. Ted, who had maintained the same expressionless face throughout, said, "A little better." I couldn't believe his restraint; his strokes had showed not the slightest lack of confidence for the last fifteen balls.

"What differences did you notice?" I asked.

"Well, I think I was taking my racket back a bit lower toward the end," Ted answered.

"Tell me, Ted, on a scale of one to ten how much change do you feel occurred in your forehand from beginning to end?"

"Oh, about two or three."

"What do you think?" I asked the audience.

"Ten!" came the unanimous response.

In short, it proved as difficult for Ted to be aware of the improvement in his forehand as it had been to perceive the hitch in his swing.

Broadcasting Our Self-Image

People enjoy telling others about the images they form of themselves, for doing so serves to strengthen one's identity with the image. The more we persuade others to believe in our picture of ourselves, the harder it is to break free. Another reason why people are so ready to broadcast the negative aspects of their image is that they hope to decrease people's expectations and dispel the pressure of trying to live up to them.

Thus, Mary, playing a match with June, says as soon as they walk on the court, "I've really been hitting my backhand badly lately. Also I haven't played at all for the last week, so I won't be very good today." This kind of opening gambit is common and understandable—and sometimes it even works. Mary feels less pressure, and consequently will probably hit her first few backhands better than she or her opponent expected. This makes her feel good, but then a problem arises: she can't allow herself to continue hitting good backhands because it will blow her image and June will think she's a liar. This is why many players who exaggerate their weaknesses and play a little better than they thought they would remain forever at a level of mediocrity.

The power of others' expectations of us can be an enormous influence. If people expect us to play well, we do tend to play better—unless, of course, our negative self-image is dominant. One of the most important pitfalls for an Inner Game instructor to avoid is not to be fooled by students' distortions in self-image. Many of them waste a lot of energy telling me how bad they are (and a few how good they are), but my job is to remain focused on what is really happening in front of me, to perceive an individual at some stage of development as a tennis player and help to remove the unnecessary restrictions on his or her potential.

Distortion No. 3: Mistaking Form for Essence

A third major way that Self 1 distorts self-image is by mistaking one's performance at a given moment for one's true potential. When a player thinks that because he hits a bad shot he has a bad backhand, he is identifying with his performance and confusing who he is with what he has done. The next step is usually to value himself in accordance with the value of his backhand.

For most of my life I was imprisoned by the proposition that my worth as a human being could be measured by my performance. In order to be worthy of respect and love I felt that I had to perform up to certain expectations. When I succeeded, Self 1 would feel good; if I didn't, it would make me feel miserable. The truth is that I am what I am; my essential nature is changeless. Of course, there is also a part of me which *does* change, and it operates best when I remember who I really am and don't identify with the ups and down of my performance.

To clarify the difference between essence and form, let's take a look at a flower. If the rose had grown to the point of having a stem and only one leaf, its Self 1 might look around at other roses and feel that it wasn't really a rose because it had no petals. Self 1 might become so anxious about this and try so hard to progress that it would interfere with its own growth. But without Self 1 a rose is a rose is a rose, from seed to bloom to seed. Its essence is no different —only its form as that changeless essence expresses itself.

How does this relate to my tennis? I remember that I am not my tennis. Rather, my game is a result of who I am, plus the interferences of who I *think* I am. My tennis, my book, my relationship with my wife don't define who I am; who I am is what defines my experience. By playing tennis I can learn something about who I am, but it cannot increase my value. I am, have been and always will be of immeasurable value merely because I am human and am part of life expressing itself.

This truth is easy to forget when my habits of mind and those of people around me tell me otherwise. But as it becomes easier to remember, one develops a sense of whole-ness which dissolves the power of Self 1's habits.

The Tournament at Claremont. Two years ago I decided to play in a tournament in the "thirty-five and over" division in Claremont, California. Though I hadn't been on the court except to teach students for some months, I wanted to experi-ence competition again. On the day of my first match, I noticed that I wasn't at all nervous, as I had expected to be. I simply went about business as usual and then drove with Sally the fifty miles to Claremont. It wasn't until we arrived at the club that I noticed the first sign of nerves. "Sally, my palms are sweating a bit," I remarked with objective interest.

As I went to look at the draw some people recognized me, and I realized for the first time that they knew I had written *The Inner Game of Tennis* and would be observing my tennis not only to evaluate *me,* but also to judge the Inner Game itself on the basis of how I played. I began to feel an added pressure.

Warming up for my first match I felt calm, but the instant it started I began to play very differently. I didn't feel at all as I usually do when giving an Inner Game lesson; instead, it was as if I were back in junior competition or in a varsity match at college. It was an entirely different me. Where did Mr. Cool Inner Game go? I wondered. I struggled, felt tight, missed some easy shots and started playing safe. Then I tried doing 'bounce-hit' with myself, and though my timing was still off, my shakiness began to vanish as the set ended 7–5 in my favor.

In the second set I decided that I was tired of playing like a scared chicken, and that at least I'd have some fun and hit every ball courageously. I played much better and did enjoy myself more, but so did my opponent, and he won the set 6–4. I was much more at ease with myself, but I still felt a little like an orphan who didn't really know who he was. Between sets all I could say to Sally was, "I'm not sure who I am out there, but it's not the Inner Game pro!" I was becoming aware that this was just one more role which could come and go like any other.

All Sally said was, "Why don't you center yourself? Do some meditation before going out for the third set."

I did, and during the final set I felt less anxiety and more energy. I won 6–2, but was still playing below my potential, and as the match ended I was already beginning to worry about my next opponent, the number four seed. I knew it would be a tough match, that it was scheduled for court 1, and that I would have to play a lot better to win or to successfully defend the reputation of the Inner Game— which was by far the greater pressure.

During the first two sets in the second match I worked only on my concentration. I calmed my mind, stayed as attentive as I could and began to feel more like an Inner Game player. I could observe the quality of my tennis improving as my self-image changed.

After splitting two hard-fought sets, we were both quite tired. There had been no more than a fifteen-minute break between my first and second match, and I wasn't used to such grueling competition. Before the third set we had a five-minute break, and again I told Sally that though I felt more like "myself" I still wasn't at home on the court and still lacked any sense of who I was out there. I meditated, attempted to center myself and then went out to play the third set.

By then it was dusk, and the lights had been turned on. I had difficulty seeing the ball in these conditions, lost the first game and was down 0–40 on my serve. But at this point my attention was not on losing or on the reactions of the crowd; I was concentrating on the ball during play and practicing meditation in between. I distinctly began to feel an energy building inside me, and I knew exactly what it was: That's who I am! I'm that energy expressing itself through this body! It's beautiful, aware, fast and accurate. It's not a bit worried about Tim Gallwey's image or the image of the Inner Game. It's perfect, and all I have to do is let it out!

And that's what I did. My tennis changed radically in that instant; I felt as fresh as if I'd just walked onto the court and had no self-doubt. I won the next five points and my serve. When I reached 0–40 on his next serve, I didn't let up as I normally might have, but went all out for the next point and won it. During the rest of the set I lost only half a dozen points, and most of those because my opponent hit winners. I was playing out of my mind.

As we shook hands afterwards, my opponent looked at me in disbelief, as if to say, "Where did that come from?" I told him I was as surprised as he was. Sally said only, "That was really beautiful." Still out of my mind, I said innocently, "Wow, it really was!" as if speaking about someone else. The experience of fulfillment inside me was exhilarating; I had let out everything that was in me.

Naturally, on the way home that evening Self 1 intruded: "If you can play like that again tomorrow, you'll beat the number one seed and be in the finals." Instead of dismissing the thought, I entertained it and reasoned to Sally that I could beat the seasoned Australian player in the semifinals, even though I hadn't been practicing, if I just identified myself with the energy inside me. Though I finally caught myself and realized that Self 1 was sneaking back, the next day I was never able to regain the spontaneity of that last set for more than a few points at a time. I played better than usual, but never played out of my mind long enough to carry me through the tough games. Losing 6–4, 6–4, I made a respectable showing, but knew that I hadn't been entirely willing to let go; Self 1 was still alive and well and looking out for its image. During the tournament I had gone through almost an entire cycle with Self 1: I had been dominated by it, had broken free for a time and then had let it possess me again. I would continue working on the Inner Game.

One might wonder what Self 1 gains out of creating and maintaining self-images which don't conform to reality, and why it is afraid to break its image barriers. One quality its tactics achieve is a sense of knowing who it is, a sense of being right. It may be a false sense of identity, but at least it makes the future predictable—and more than anything else Self 1 wants life to be predictable. It is afraid of the changing and unlimited nature of experience, and afraid of not being in control, especially over oneself or others close to oneself. Therefore it hurriedly forms concepts which promote a sense of permanence and stability. Self 1 would rather feel that it is a lousy tennis player and be able to predict its performance than to be surprised and not know what to expect. It solidifies this image by telling others that it is bad, thus encouraging them to imprison it as well with the power of their expectations. Hence, when Self 1 sees that something—genuine growth, learning, change—may threaten its concept of the way things are, it expends a lot of energy making sure that it and others conform to its expectations.

This effort that we employ in image-forming and image-maintenance robs us of the energy we need for the goals of Self 2: growing, learning and expressing oneself. Self 2 is not at all static or predictable. It won't be pigeonholed in tidy conceptual categories or be limited in any way. Its nature is to change and to express a variety of abilities and talents without ever being totally defined. Self 1's desire to limit, control and define runs counter to Self 2's nature. But though Self 1 wants to limit life and make it manageable, it doesn't have the power to do so except in its own imagination; it can only *think* it knows and controls, and in that way hide from the recognition of the superiority of Self 2. Of course, Self 1 can also pretend that it can't do things which it can and that it can do things which it can't, and in that sense it is quite powerful. When we identify with our self-concepts, we in fact start acting according to Self 1 roles and become limited and predictable.

Self-Definition—a Barrier to Learning

This raises an important point about learning or growing in general. Both are involved with change, whereas self-concept is concerned with the status quo. One way out of this contradiction is to accept a concept of yourself which allows for change; that is, to think of yourself as a human being in the constant process of change. This step is usually taken by people who want to encourage growth in themselves. But it is difficult to allow oneself to change rapidly, to give up one's sense of permanence and precious self-image. People who make a goal out of "growing" or "searching" often allow themselves merely the illusion of change and of nearing their goal.

Because Self 1 has such a hard time handling change, human beings find it difficult to let themselves change. We may adopt new acts, but we cling to the deep core of our self-image. Often the more we alter our appearance, the more attached we become to our concept of self. I know only one way out of this dilemma: forget about making an effort to grow, to change, to learn, and instead put your energies into perceiving your essence and discovering that part of yourself which *doesn't* change—not because it's a useful concept, but because it's who you really are. The closer one comes to the center of oneself, the closer one approaches that which doesn't change—that which, in fact, produces growth. Then change is no longer frightening and takes place automatically, because it is our nature.

Consider what it would be like to be a caterpillar changing into a butterfly. That is a very dramatic growth, requiring a lot of new learning in a very short period of time. If the caterpillar had a Self 1, it would panic as it left the security and tangibility of the earth for the limitless ambience of the air. In worrying about losing its feet and beautiful fur it would resist its alteration and probably take forever to express its potential as a butterfly. One can imagine that the only way the Self 1 of a caterpillar could handle this transformation would be to identify with whatever part of it didn't change during its transformation. To all appearances it is becoming a totally new creature, but is there something which remains constant that it can cling to? Yes: its life. The life animating the caterpillar is the same as that of the butterfly; it merely expresses itself in two different forms. If the caterpillar could focus on the life within itself, on its essence, the transformation would be as easy as changing clothes.

Self-Discovery versus Self-Definition

The subject of self-image is complex, and my understanding of it is only beginning, but one thing that has made a great deal of difference in my life has become clear to me. I now realize that there is an enormous difference between Self 1's process of self-definition—that is, the creation and maintenance of concepts about yourself—and the process called self-discovery. When I play the game of trying to define myself, I am constantly comparing myself with others, measuring myself in terms of higher and lower, better and worse, more right or more wrong than others. Or I may measure myself against internal standards and expectations of how I *should* be. My sense of self-worth rises and falls continuously, on the basis of my performance and of how harshly I judge myself at any given moment.

The process of self-discovery could hardly be more different. When I am able to achieve this state, I do not assume that I have to become anything that I already am not, and so my only task is to explore and express whatever it is I happen to be. There is no need to imprison myself in a cell of my own making or into the mold of others' expectations. Rather, my job is to let go of the concepts and limiting images which prevent me from perceiving and expressing my greatest potential. I don't want this potential to be any different than it actually is; I only want to fulfill that which is already there. And of all the potentials I may possess, I most want to realize the one I hold in common with every other individual: to know what it is to be human, and to express the essence of that which is unique to our species and held in common by all of us.

7
The Will to Win

As the reader may now have discovered, the organization of this book moves from "outside" to "inside." The two chapters following the introductory one dealt with increasing awareness of the ball, an external object; Chapters 4 and 5 were concerned with awareness of the body in motion; and Chapter 6 discussed increasing one's awareness of the self inside the body. This chapter will focus on the core of the self: the will. At each level one principle has been paramount: *increasing one's awareness of what is* facilitates beneficial and natural change. But at its deepest level increasing awareness of our will can bring about changes in all the other levels— in the way we view ourselves, how we move our bodies and the way we perceive events. A change in the direction of one's will—that is, in one's basic motivations—is the most powerful form of human change.

First I'd like to clear up a common misconception. Some people have assumed that the Inner Game means *not* striving to win, *not* making an effort, avoiding serious competition, and simply playing for the fun of it. But this is not the goal of the Inner Game. Rather, its purpose is to help those who practice it to overcome obstacles which prevent the fullest expression of one's potential. Overcoming obstacles, whether inner or outer, requires effort, and no goal is attained without it. Similarly, no game is won without the will to win, the single-minded desire to conquer whatever obstacles exist between a player—of a game, of a career, of life itself—and his goal. The more difficult the obstacles, the greater the demand on one's effort and perseverance. This is a universal and most natural process. The plant makes an effort to grow. It has a will to sink its roots into the earth and then to express itself upwards toward the sun. If there is a rock in the way, the plant will try to go around it. The will of nature is to fulfill its natural purpose.

Thus, effort and will are necessary both in life and in the playing of any game. But how does one go about strengthening his determination to reach a goal? What is the relationship between the will to win and *letting it happen,* between necessary effort and *trying too hard*? How do you overcome the self-defeating anxiety and overcontrol that are the by-products of believing that winning is important?

To gain insight into the problems that people face with their will to win, on or off the tennis court, let us consider the nature of the will itself. "Will" refers to the motivating principle behind action, and has two essential components: a *direction* and a *strength.* The direction is the target of the desire; the strength refers to its intensity and duration. Winning, the goal usually desired by tennis players, is a component of direction, and the strength of that will to win can be measured by the amount of energy an individual is willing to expend to achieve its objective, or by the amount of resistance from internal or external sources that the will was able to conquer in order to reach its goal.

Will Vectors

The two basic components of any desire can be represented in the same way as vectors in physics. A vector is a directed line segment representing a physical quantity, such as velocity, that has magnitude and direction in space. The angle of the vector represents the velocity's direction and the length of the line represents its magnitude. Take, for example, a boat whose engine is propelling it north at ten miles per hour against a southern current of speed two miles per hour, at the same time while a prevailing wind is acting against the boat from the east at four miles an hour. The vector diagram showing these velocities would look like this:

The resultant velocity of the boat would cause it to travel in a northwesterly direction at a velocity of less than nine miles per hour.

Our various wills act in the same way. Take a player who wants to win but also has a desire to look graceful while doing so, and at the same time is afraid to play too well for fear of shattering his self-image or of raising other people's expectations. To make it simple, let's assume that he places 50 percent of his effort into winning and 20 percent into looking graceful, while the remaining 30 percent is wasted on his fear. A vector diagram of this player's three desires would look something like this:

The length of each arrow represents the strength of the given desire at the moment, and its angle represents the direction in which the will is acting. When these forces are all acting simultaneously, the resulting diagram might look like this:

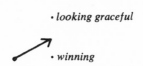

Less than 40 percent of this player's energies are acting effectively, and they are expended in a direction somewhere between winning and looking graceful. An observer might say that this player was not really determined to win, and that he had a weak will. But if all his energies were channeled toward winning, without any concern for looking good and without fear, his will vector would look like this:

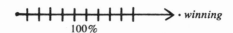

100%

Now his play would be much more effective and his single-minded determination very apparent.

Many players feel that they don't have sufficient will to win and try to strengthen their determination by gritting their teeth and trying too hard. This usually leads to frustration, and eventually even to giving up the game. But the primary thesis of this chapter is that the necessary will to reach one's goals lies within all of us, and that the task of the player of the Inner Game is to discover what winning really is—that is, to discover what he really wants. The reason we often have less motivation than we think we need to reach a given goal is not that we are weak-willed, but that we are confused about that goal; we have many objectives at the same time, and our energies are dispersed. Self 2 has a strong desire to know itself and to express its full potential, but if most of our energies are being expended on various Self 1 assignments, many of which may be contradictory, there will be relatively little energy left for Self 2. Then a person finds himself easily distracted and without the necessary drive to overcome difficult obstacles. When you are really clear about what you want, it is usually not difficult to organize your resources effectively to attain your goal; in fact, it is done quite automatically by Self 2.

The Inner Game approach to strengthening your will lies first in clarifying what you really want—that is, what "winning" really is for you—and then sacrificing the other, less important desires that distract you from your true purpose. When a player focuses on his Self 2 motivation and lets go of all of Self 1's distractions, effort becomes easy. Then you can proceed toward your goal just as a river flows toward the ocean, with a strong and natural determination, overcoming all obstacles without apparent force, winning without a hint of trying too hard.

Enough of theory. Let us return to the pragmatic approach in examining competition.

Confusion about Goals in Competition

Competitive games offer a fascinating opportunity to perceive the confusion about winning which exists in the minds of most players, and how that confusion affects their determination. Although few tennis players recognize this confusion about goals when competing, most are prey to it. For instance, if I ask a group whether they prefer opponents who are better or worse players than they are, 95 percent usually say that they like to compete against someone who is better. But when I ask, "Imagine that you are now in a match against this better player and that he is leading 3–2 on his serve at deuce; as you wait for the serve, are you hoping that he's going to get his serve in, or that he'll hit it into the net?" with an embarrassed laugh most of the group will admit that in fact they are hoping for a double fault, or at least for an easy setup.

Isn't this changing one's mind? When we arrange a match, we want a strong opponent, but once we are playing we want him to double-fault. This is nothing more than confusion about one's goals. Obviously something is more important to us than winning or we would choose opponents we could beat easily and would win every time.

When we compete, we generally recognize that our chances of improving and of learning will be increased if we play against someone better who can give us stiff competition. But once in the game we forget that we are playing with the intention of learning and improving and begin thinking that winning is all-important. Starting with the motive of wanting to improve, we are sidetracked into the Self 1 goal of proving that we are better than our opponent. "Proving" and "improving" are two very different directions for one's will and energies. When the natural desire of Self 2 to express its full potential is subsumed by Self 1's desire to prove something, anxiety appears—and with it the overcontrol and tightness that often leads to losing.

There is a crucial distinction between the reason for playing a competitive game and the goal of the game itself. The objective of the game is to win, but the reason for playing the game in the first place is usually different—to learn, to improve, to express one's full potential, for enjoyment or exercise, and so forth. It is these benefits that Self 2 looks for when he arranges a match, whereas the rewards of winning the game itself are utterly different. When a player can clearly perceive the relationship between his reason for playing and his desire to win, it becomes easy to organize his energies and resources effectively to attain what he *really* wants.

The Nature of Competition

Then what is the purpose of competing beyond determining who is better? Does Self 2 have a motive in competition? Perhaps we can clarify this subject by considering a simple form of competition between the right and left hands. Letting your two hands represent opposing players, center them between your knees and give them opposing goals. Winning for the right hand means pushing the left hand past the left knee, and vice versa. Play will be continuous. Ready, set, go! Start pushing.

Let us assume that after some time the right hand wins. Is your response to this to applaud it, treat it more tenderly and view it with greater respect? And do you disdain your left hand for being a loser? Of course not; yet it is analogous to the way we often treat winners and losers, even in our family. But let us look again at this competition to discover if anything of value may have resulted from it. Is there any real value for Self 2 in such a contest?

Of course there is. If you push your hands against each other for five minutes a day, each of them increases its strength in this simple isometric exercise. But what would happen if the left hand said, "I don't believe in compeition; it's just an ego trip. Winning isn't important, so I won't push hard." Then the right hand would win easily, and neither hand would benefit from the competition.

In other words, competition for Self 2 is essentially a form of cooperation in which each side benefits by making an effort *to oppose* the other. Each needs the other's resistance. Thus, Self 2 wants the first serve of its opponent to be a good one because it is easier for it to express itself with a challenge, and the greater the challenge, the more Self 2 can use the full extent of its potential. The resistance Self 2 encounters is what encourages it to exceed its previous limits, calling forth its greatest concentration, skill and determination. In this way Self 2 increases its self-knowledge and extends the range of its capabilities.

But Self 2 benefits from competition only in proportion to the effort it expends to win. Neither right nor left hand will grow stronger if they don't try to push the other back. However, it is not the hand that wins that necessarily increases its strength the most. If the right hand won but employed only 60 percent of its potential to do so, it will not increase its strength as much as the weaker hand which used 90 percent of its capacity. The real value in this competition depends on how much each hand directs its energies toward winning *during* the contest, rather than in winning itself.

What this means is that there are two kinds of winning in competition: that which takes place in the game, and the winning of the game itself. Each player must decide which is the more important to him—that is, which game he is really playing.

The Nature and Use of Games

The real value in playing any game lies in the fact that it is a simulation of life. Games are designed to be *like* life situations, but without the "real" consequences resulting from mistakes. It is because of the make-believe nature of games that they are such perfect learning situations, for they allow the individual the chance to experiment and exercise his capabilities without worrying about *really* losing anything. For example, Monopoly is a simulation of the real estate profession. The money you win or lose is worthless, the jail you go to is a symbolic one, and at the end, whether you won or lost and played well or badly, all the hotels you had on "Boardwalk" go back in the little box they came from. Still, during the game you throw your dice, make decisions and reap consequences very much as in real life. The fun experienced is not simulated but very real, and so is the exercise of your decision-making ability and wheeling and dealing. Hence, players can learn a lot about themselves during the game. With their "pretend" rewards and punishments, games allow a person to handle himself under mock pressures and to learn skills and lessons which can help him in his life beyond the game.

When Self 2 plays, it enters this "pretend" reality, obeys its rules and pursues its goals. But it is playing for a different reason—perhaps to learn something about who and what it really is. The confusion comes when Self 1 gets lost in the game and starts thinking that winning this simulation of life is truly important. Instead of experiencing a simulation pressure it experiences the real thing; instead of acting worried, it becomes actually scared. That's when Self 1 tightens and chokes. It is the confusing of the "pretend" nature of games with real life that causes eleven-year-old boys to cry their hearts out after losing a match, or grown men to be depressed for a week because they were beaten in a challenge match. For these individuals the learning aspect of games is largely lost.

But if we can remember our real motive for playing in the first place, we can go all out to win while in the match, yet never fool ourselves that winning is more than a make-believe goal. Such a player can be happy while winning crucial points, and in feeling his adrenaline flow when his back is against the wall; but he never forgets that the game is only a simulation of real life. The greater the pressure, the more he likes it; the stiffer the competition, the more the challenge. He is in a position to go all out and to take risks because he is always conscious of the fact that there is nothing real to lose. In this condition he actually plays better, learns more and has more fun. He is like a good actor onstage, able to involve himself in all the emotions and actions of the drama without ever forgetting that it is, after all, only a play. Imagine an actor who so completely forgets his real identity and purpose in being onstage that he begins to think that his role is life itself; he would be as confused as the game player who forgets the difference between a game and life.

Self 2's inner game welcomes external obstacles in outer games in order to overcome the internal barriers hindering its development and highest form of self-expression, and thereby to attain freedom. In contrast, Self 1 seeks to avoid difficulties. It doesn't want to explore its limits; rather, it hopes to establish an image, a reputation. It assumes that the real benefits come from winning the game itself, not in conquering internal difficulties. Self 2 attaches only secondary importance to winning the outer game, but it believes that playing it as well as it can is important to its primary goal of winning the inner game. Hence, Self 2 expends its maximum effort when engaged in any outer game, and focuses that effort on winning any competition. It plays by the rules of the game, but uses the simulation of life for its own higher purposes.

Is Self 2's Motivation Practical?

One may ask whether Self 2's welcoming of difficulties and trying to attain its full potential is as practical as Self 1's motivation to win the game itself. Which motivation achieves the best results in the outer-game sense? Consider George, who views winning the last point as his primary goal. His will is focused on an objective whose attainment is not completely in his control, but is dependent on the efforts of his opponent as well. If both players set their sights on winning the outer game, one of them will be disappointed.

When a person desires something he may not get, he becomes anxious. Anxiety always appears when you seek an objective not entirely within your control, or wish to avoid something that is partially dependent on the will of others. The degree of anxiety is in proportion to how much you want something, and is inversely proportionate to the extent of your control. The anxiety experienced by George becomes an obstacle which interferes with his performance; while he worries about winning or losing, he loses his concentration and determination. Harry, on the other hand, who decides that what is most important is the benefits that accrue to him during the competition, in accordance with the amount and quality of his effort, is far better off. His goal is entirely in his control, and nobody or no event outside himself can prevent him from making his maximum effort. He is in control and therefore experiences no anxiety. His purpose in competing is to do his best to win, and even if he finds that he is not reaching his full potential the choice is in his hands to overcome the inner and outer difficulties of the situation. In short, he cannot be denied the benefits resulting from his efforts.

Now, how will Harry fare in competition? Of course he won't win every outer game he plays, but if he consistently attains his goal of making maximum effort, he will play as well as he possibly can in each match and therefore will have as good a record as possible for him in the outer game. By placing priority on the inner game, Harry maximizes his chances of winning the outer game. By placing priority on winning the outer game, George unnecessarily risks losing both. Most athletes play with a mixture of Self 1 and Self 2 motives, but those who most closely realize their potential concentrate their energies on the moment and don't allow themselves to be distracted by Self 1's fears of losing.

Let's take another example, this time from a noncompetitive situation. When a player goes out to practice, his motivation in doing so is all-important. If he is seeking to heighten his self-image or to prove himself, he is apt to practice those shots he already hits well. He will tend to run around his weak backhand, to avoid difficult shots. But when his motive is to improve his game and expand his possibilities, he works on his weaknesses and welcomes what seems difficult. As a consequence he improves, just as the player who strives for the appearance of grace may also succeed. Both may receive what they want from their practice, but each arrives at a different goal and different rewards. To repeat: each player must ask himself which game he wants to play.

Switching Games at Kalamazoo

It's easy to switch one's goals in the middle of a match. In an instant a player can shift from Self 2 to Self 1 motivation, and it will make all the difference in his performance and in what he actually attains. My most vivid memory of shifting back and forth between Self 1's desire to win and Self 2's control occurred when I was fifteen years old and playing in the National Junior Championships at Kalamazoo, Michigan. Even today I am still learning from that experience some of the basic lessons about the relationship between letting go and determination to reach an objective.

The day before going East for the tournament I was asked by my coach, John Gardiner, whether or not I expected to win. Though I knew I had talent and though I worked hard on my game, I had never really considered myself a winner. I seemed to play my best when I was behind, and was known for startling comebacks, but as soon as I was in a position to beat someone I thought a better player I usually lost concentration, let up and blew the match. So I tried to give an honest, objective answer to my coach's question. "Well, I doubt if I'll win," I said. "There are a lot of players tougher than I in the tournament, certainly a lot with more experience."

Gardiner looked disappointed, and said, "Well, if you don't have the will to win, you probably won't." He turned and walked away, leaving me perplexed.

I try hard, I thought to myself. I practice long hours every day. I get nervous before matches and discouraged when I lose, but I sure do want to win. Yet I know that what he says is true: if I really wanted to win, I wouldn't let my opponent off the hook when I'm ahead. I can remember thinking that I really wanted to win, but being baffled by the problem of making myself want something more than I already did.

By the time I arrived in Kalamazoo, I had reached a kind of resolution to my problem. I was then going through a religious phase in my adolescence, and I decided to put the question of winning and losing entirely in God's hands. Before every match I prayed, "Whatever you want, God, is okay with me. It's up to you."

Of my first three matches, two were on the grandstand court, the first time I had ever experienced the pressure of an audience. I played some of the best tennis of my life, each time beating players whom I honestly thought were better than I. By then I was in the round of sixteen against Alan Silverman, the seventh-ranked player and the following year's national champion. Again our match was scheduled for the grandstand court. I was nervous, but said my prayer and astounded myself as well as the crowd, which was cheering for me as the underdog, by winning the first set 6–3. Alan then astounded me in the second by changing tactics and rushing the net at every opportunity. I was overwhelmed, and lost the set 6–0.

During the break a stranger from the crowd whispered to me the advice to lob when Alan came up to net. I took it as a commandment from God, and even though it didn't work in the first few games of the third set, I persisted. Soon I found myself ahead 5–3 on my serve. One more game was all I needed. It's all in God's hands, I said to myself as I began serving. I played well and soon the score was 40–15—match point. For the first time I became fully aware that I could win the match. Just one more point, I thought. I am actually going to beat the seventh-ranked player in the country! I grew excited, and can still remember every instant of the next minute of my life. Thank you very much, God, for your help, I said to myself. I can take it from here! I am quoting exactly my thought as I walked over to serve in the deuce court.

I'll try to ace him, I said to myself on my first match point. My first serve hit the net cord. I'll hit the next one hard; he'll be expecting an easy second serve and I'll end the match with an ace, I thought. "Out. Double fault. Forty–thirty," the umpire called out. Looking into the ad court, I felt nervous. I'll serve and rush the net this time. Maybe he'll be nervous and miss his passing shot, I said to myself. My first serve landed deep in the backhand court, and Alan returned it with a very wide and low backhand shot. Rushing the net, I had no time to think. I reached out for it, caught it in front of me with an open face and sliced it at a sharp angle only a few inches over the net and about a foot from the sideline. It was an almost perfect shot and I doubted that Alan could even get to it, but moved over to my right just in case. He raced up to the ball, sliding on the slow red clay with arm outstretched, and caught it just before it bounced for the second time, but with only enough force to lob it slowly up to my forehand at shoulder height. I was a mere four feet from the net and six feet from the side line, while Alan was just across the net from me, so that the entire lefthand court was wide open for my shot. The ball seemed to take forever to reach me, but when it finally did I hit it firmly into the net.

I had lost my second match point; the score was deuce, and my heart was in my shoes. Though I fought hard for the rest of the set, I felt that I had lost my opportunity; Alan finally won 10–8, and I was left wondering why I was a loser. I had to go back to my coach and tell him that he was right: I just didn't have the will to win.

The Will to Win versus Letting It Happen

My match at Kalamazoo symbolizes the dilemma between determination to reach a goal and letting it happen. In retrospect it is easy to see what occurred. First, though I didn't realize it at the time, the prayer was a way of rejecting Self 1 and allowing Self 2 to play the game. Having let go of concern about winning the outer game, my energies were focused on reaching my full potential; I was concentrated, consistent, scrappy, didn't miss easy shots and was, during the first two matches and for most of the third, out of my mind.

Then, on the verge of beating Alan, I began to entertain thoughts about winning, to taste the fruits of victory. Self 1 reappeared, and I started fantasizing about being in the quarter finals, perhaps even winning the tournament, and about how impressed people would be with this unknown player from California. Instead of dismissing those thoughts, I said to myself, Thanks, God, I'll take it from here. With those thoughts of winning there came a certain excitement I hadn't felt before, but also a certain nervousness. I realized, too, that I might blow the match. I wanted to make sure of winning, and I wanted credit for the victory. When winning became the most important goal, losing took on added importance as well. It was the fear of losing which was responsible for my poor judgment in attempting a second-serve ace on the first match point, and for the overtrying and tensing up that made me miss the easy volley on the second. After wasting both opportunities, I was back *in* my mind. Discouragement at choking became an additional obstacle, and so did the realization that I had taken the match out of God's hands and back into my own. For the rest of the match I was overcautious and trying extra hard to redeem myself, and eventually fought my way to defeat. The opponent inside and the one outside proved too much.

From this match I learned for the first time that my will to win was stronger if my mind was detached from the consequences. It was the first fumbling step toward the Inner Game.

Self 2 Effort versus Self 1 Trying

Even players who recognize that they play better when they "don't really care" about the results are often afraid that if they don't try hard they will rob themselves of incentive and become *careless*. If a player gives up Self 1's concern about winning or losing, looking graceful and so forth, what is it that *will* motivate him?

Sometimes I suggest to a student, "Don't try to hit this ball well."

He or she looks at me anxiously and asks, "Do you want me to try to hit it badly?"

"No. Don't try to hit it well *or* badly. Don't try at all."

"Then I might not even hit the ball at all. I really don't know what will happen."

"Exactly. We'll find out."

By letting go of all Self 1's hangups, we can become more aware of what Self 2 wants to do when it is given permission to express its will without interference. This is the basic Inner Game experiment: Is there anything within us that really cares, that makes effort? Who is it, and what does it care about? How competent and intelligent is it? These questions can only be answered by the individual doing the experiment.

My own experience is that when trying ends and Self 1's concerns are forgotten, a strong motivating principle remains. Awkwardness and overtightness diminish, and an exquisitely economic use of energy emerges when Self 2's motivation is given free rein. It is this Self 2 will that is responsible for the apparent magic in the curative power of awareness discussed in preceding chapters. Theoretically, a person with a perfectly still mind who is totally concentrated on the trajectory of the ball might just remain aware of the ball as it bounces and let it go by without trying to hit it. But in fact when Self 1 is absorbed in *seeing* the ball rather than in "trying," effort is still made, and the ball is returned, usually with more power and accuracy and less strain.

When doing the body awareness exercises described in Chapter 5, remember that it is the will of Self 2 which causes the decrease in overtightness, or that makes the pain disappear when the student is simply paying attention to it without trying to change it. Likewise, when one aims at a target without trying to hit it, balls come closer and closer to the target as one observes nonjudgmentally where they are landing. Awareness doesn't cure by itself; it simply gives Self 2 the feedback necessary for it to follow its intention. In most cases Self 2 is quite happy to play tennis if you let it. If the game is to hit the ball over the net, it will express itself accordingly; if the objective is to win the last point, it will focus its efforts in that direction. It wants to win—but it also knows that losing can't hurt it.

Effort versus Trying When Playing under Pressure

All games have their moments of truth, those crucial points where everything you do counts. Tie breakers in tennis are an example, as are overtimes in basketball, the three-two pitch in the ninth inning with the score tied in baseball, and the last few minutes of a close football game. During these moments of pressure the player is really tested, and it is then that Self 1 is most apt to try to regain control. It is when winning or losing is most imminent that it is easiest for fear to take hold. Think what goes through the mind of the golfer on the pro tour who has played four rounds and is finally on the eighteenth hole, eight feet from the cup, and putting for a birdie to win the tournament. What makes this putt harder than the same putt during the first round? His mind's reactions to his situation, of course. The player must overcome his mind to hole out a putt he is fully capable of sinking.

These pressure situations are one of the most valuable parts of games. They simulate the tensions of real life, and such practice in keeping one's mind concentrated and totally in the present is valuable when we meet more important crises. But the ability to stay concentrated and remain under the superior control of Self 2 can also be tested in more relaxed situations, and the control gained will become apparent in more critical situations. Self 2 enjoys pressure and will rise to the occasion, but it never confuses game pressure with the real thing. The only real opponent it knows is within. (Note: there is an interesting sidelight to this subject. Many players who become nervous and distracted under the pressure of a game respond calmly and efficiently in real emergencies. When they have to be effective, they rely on Self 2 and simply don't indulge themselves in the fears of Self 1.)

What increases pressure in games? To a certain extent it is the circumstances of the game itself, but generally it is due even more to the situation surrounding the match. Pressure tends to mount if other participants or spectators mistake the game for real life, evaluating the player himself according to how he plays or whether he wins or loses. It is extremely difficult to remember one's inner goal when those around you are assuming that the outer game is all-important. Remembering one's own inner game under such pressure is one more challenge.

When external rewards, psychological or physical, are offered to the winner of a competition, it can act as an incentive for both sides to make a maximum effort, and therefore each will benefit. But there is a danger. If the competitors become so intrigued by the incentive that they forget about the intrinsic rewards of the competition itself, they forget what games are all about in the first place and winning the reward becomes the only objective. Then learning is minimized, joy is lost, anxiety grows, and sooner or later excellence diminishes.

This switch of allegiance from inner to outer rewards is a crucial factor influencing many areas of people's lives. As children we began the learning process motivated more by the rewards inherent in learning itself—by the natural joy of discovery rather than by the practical benefits of knowledge of one's world. But in order to increase concentration and effort, as well as to influence the direction of learning, parents and teachers offer physical and psychological rewards for excellence. In these circumstances it becomes easy to grow so dependent on the external rewards that we become confused about our goals. It is simpler to chase A's instead of understanding, to pursue reputation and praise instead of knowledge. Then we lose touch with Self 2's motivation. Praise and recognition are natural by-products of excellence, but they are dubious goals in themselves.

The way we train children in schools is largely repeated in their subsequent lives. As workers we tend to believe that we should expect little benefit from the job itself, and that work is done solely for the external rewards earned—the pay, recognition, status and so on. Many employers and employees could benefit greatly by paying more attention to the neglected intrinsic rewards which can and should come from the job itself. If the individual receives no satisfaction from his work for its own sake, he dies internally, a condition which no financial reward can justly compensate.

It should be recognized that professional athletes play for very large financial rewards. In these cases competitive games often become equated with real life, since they are the source of livelihood, and here the pressures of game and of life become one and the same. But even playing professionals have to make an effort not to become too attached to winning or losing. They may value winning the external rewards more than the Inner Game, but if winning becomes *too* important, they are apt to sabotage their efforts with anxiety. The best professionals are those who maintain their full potential under pressure, but can walk away in defeat without really losing. I suspect that the best professionals in any sport do not work primarily for financial reward. Money becomes only a part of the game, a measure of performance. One can speculate about a perspective in which one's entire life becomes a game with a more permanent reality. If such a view becomes real for a player, he will be able to handle all life situations with the same abandonment and skill he achieves in sport.

Pressure, which is always experienced in the mind, is not necessarily a bad experience that should be avoided, because sometimes it helps us to attain new heights. But I have found it valuable to ask myself two questions whenever faced with pressure either in a game or in life. First, what do I really win by winning? Secondly, what do I really lose by losing? If these two questions are answered honestly and penetratingly, the player (of game or of life) will find himself motivated to achieve what he really wants without the fear that will inhibit victory. Too often players are fooled into thinking that there is more to be lost and more to be won than there actually is. As a result, they are suckered into chasing Self 1's goals of praise, notoriety and approval, and into fearing loss of reputation and respect. But though such rewards are actual, do they really benefit the player? Are they truly the goal one wants to play for?

B. F. Skinner and His Pigeons

Our common tendency to be fooled into chasing rewards which ultimately don't satisfy us reminds me of an experiment conducted by B. F. Skinner, the Harvard behaviorist, on pigeons. I observed this experiment in a course I took in 1957 called Natural Science 114: The Science of Human Behavior. One day Skinner brought out his "Skinner box" with a pigeon inside, and asked the class what we wanted it to do. "Have him jump on his left foot in counterclockwise circles," challenged one of the more arrogant sophomores mockingly.

Within ten minutes, the pigeon was doing exactly that—hopping crazily in counterclockwise circles on his left foot. I was awed and a little frightened. The procedure was so simple. Skinner's cage was equipped with a light, bell and food trough, each of them triggered by a control box which he held in his hand. Skinner simply watched the random behavior of the pigeon until it showed the first element of the desired behavior—say, a weighting of the left foot. At exactly the right moment, he pushed his button, and on went the light, the bell rang, and the food trough opened. The pigeon ate and then continued its random movement until again it leaned on its left foot and again was rewarded with food. Within a few minutes the bird was spending a lot of time on its left foot, but the process had taken quite a while and at this rate it looked as if it would take Skinner hours to train the pigeon to achieve the more complicated requirement of jumping in counterclockwise circles. But now he instituted a trick: with every desired element of behavior the pigeon made, he would push another button which turned on the light and rang the bell, but *didn't* open the food trough! Thereafter the training proceeded rapidly, since it was no longer interrupted by the pigeon's eating time. The light and bell themselves, by being closely associated with the food, had become sufficient reward to get the bird to do what Skinner wanted, and within five more minutes it was hopping on its left foot in counterclockwise circles.

At that time I had only a faint glimmer of the parallel between the pigeon's fate and my own. At the beginning of the experiment the bird was getting what it really wanted: food. From its point of view, it could be said to be training Skinner to give him food simply by standing on its left foot. Both were getting what they wanted by cooperating. But soon it became clear who was playing whose game. With only a symbolic reward and no real satisfaction, the pigeon was dancing to Skinner's tune, showing itself for what it was: simply a pigeon, conned into working for a false reward.

To be sure, after some time the light and the bell would have lost their power unless reassociated with the *real* reward, the food. But it seems to be a unique attribute of human beings that they will chase symbolic rewards to the point of death without recognizing that they are missing the real thing. So the smart pigeon discriminates in every situation what winning really means for him, and continually reappraises its goals so that it doesn't exhaust itself chasing appearances.

Discriminating between Outer and Inner Goals

One individual can never tell another what is best to want, but the main point of the preceding pages is that it makes sense for players of all games to be clear about their goals. No one wants to spend a lifetime or his playing years chasing symbolic goals and missing what would really have been more satisfying. Below is a rough list of some of the rewards intrinsic to playing tennis—that is, benefits that can be attained during the game—and beside it are some of the external rewards sometimes available after winning the outer game.

DURING PLAY	AFTER WINNING
Exercise and health	Trophy or financial reward
Enjoyment	Status and recognition
Improving one's game	Pride of achievement
Developing concentration	Feeling of victory
Developing the ability to stay calm under pressure	Opportunities to play with better players
Developing self-confidence	Better self-image
Developing determination	Approval of others
Increasing one's self-knowledge	
The expression of one's potential on all levels—physical, mental, spiritual	

The above is admittedly an incomplete list because each of us finds a variety of other rewards both during and after the competition. But if we compare the two, one fact immediately becomes apparent. Only one player can win the outer game, while both can win the inner game, whose rewards are not limited or finite. Your opponent and other circumstances can prevent you from winning the outer rewards, but *only* you can prevent yourself from reaping the internal ones. To the extent that your opponent plays well, he deprives you of external victory, but nothing he does can keep you from being victorious over your own mind.

Secondly, the blessings of victory in the outer game are conditional; that is, the value of the trophy depends largely on what it means to you and others, and the worth of the financial reward depends on its amount and on the use one can make of it. The respect of others based on winning is ephemeral, especially in our culture; lose a couple of times and it vanishes. (In fact, you will be even less respected as a *fallen* hero than if you'd never been one in the first place.) Even the self-respect gained from winning is of dubious value, for it then follows that you will be deprived of self-respect when you lose. To let your self-respect depend on your performance is to ensure an unstable sense of self; you are then caught in the game of measuring your value in comparison to the performance of others—with every competitor a potential victim or possible threat.

What about the enjoyment of tennis? When do you have the most fun—during the match, afterwards, or both equally? Which lasts the longer? Which do you prefer? You may think you know the answers, but it won't do you any harm to check what you believe with the actual experience the next time you play tennis.

Here's another question that requires more subtle attention. Does the real pleasure occur for you during your stroke or not until after you see where it landed? Which do you find more satisfying? Check on this from time to time, for it is a good indicator of whether the inner game or the outer is your first priority in any given situation.

Self 1 and the Will to Lose

One of the points made in the foregoing pages is that there is really no such thing as a *weak* will to win, only a *divided* will. Self 2 may want to go one way, while Self 1 may be wandering in many other directions at the same time. In fact, it is quite possible for Self 1 to want to win and to lose simultaneously. Though we are usually much less aware of our desire to lose, we often lose when we don't have to because without being aware of it we are playing other games that are different from the winning game. A partial list of the innumerable double binds that Self 1 gets itself into because of its conflicting desires would include the following:

1. "If I win, then I'll have to live up to a higher expectation of myself next time. If I become the champion, I'll have to remain champion or disappoint myself and be criticized by others for not living up to their expectations."
2. "If I beat Harry, who really wants to win this set, he'll be angry with me." (A problem often faced between husbands and wives and fathers and sons.)
3. "If I win too much, I'll be less popular. You can't be top dog and one of the gang at the same time." (One woman told me that because she was playing much better recently

her friends were upset and made such remarks as "So you think you're getting too good for us, do you?" She didn't know which was more important to her—keeping her friendship with her fellow players, or fulfilling her desire to improve as much as she could.)

4. "I want to play well, but I don't think I really deserve to." (It's not at all unusual for Self 1 to try to punish itself for not living up to its expectations. It starts hating itself for not playing well, and then gets perverse revenge by not letting you enjoy the fruits of winning.)

5. "I want to win because it's really important for me, but I don't want to be responsible for my opponent's losing. I don't have the killer instinct; I don't want my opponent to feel as badly as I would if I lost."

6. "I'm at my best when I play out of my mind, but I also want the credit."

7. "I want to win and know that this takes all-out effort, but I don't want to lose after putting everything into it. I want to have the excuse that at least I didn't try as hard as I could because it's too painful not to win when I've made maximum effort."

Usually Self 1 sees many advantages to winning and playing well, but it also sees disadvantages to playing *too* well and winning *too* much. Making errors and losing occasionally help to lower the expectations placed on itself; help to avoid the feeling that it is a killer on the court; help to minimize the jealousy of others; help to maintain a *normal* image of itself, thereby providing a sense of continuity and identity. Most players have all these and more reasons for not playing their best. In fact, often errors are made because we *want* to make them—when our desire to miss outweighs our desire *not* to. This statement may seem hard to swallow because we have so many excuses for missing shots. For instance, "I took my eye off the ball" is easier to say than "I wanted to miss, so I took my eye off the ball." But if an error is defined as missing a shot which is within our capability, it follows that the only reason we missed is because some part of us wanted to. No one else made us take our eyes off the ball. As we come to recognize the fact of life that we are where we are because we want to be there, no matter how strong our apparent discontent, it becomes easier to resolve some of the apparent conflicts in our desires, and to allow our energies to flow more directly toward goals that we desire wholeheartedly.

Errorless Tennis

One day I was giving a lesson to Dorothy, an intermediate player. We had been doing ball-awareness and racket-awareness exercises and I had been telling her to stay focused on the ball and not worry about whether it landed in the court, but to be aware of what happened. After forty minutes of practicing letting go, Dorothy was relaxed and flowing in her movements; her fear and overcautiousness were dissolving, and there was no *trying* left.

Suddenly I felt an abrupt change in my voice. "Now don't miss another shot!" I commanded. "There's no need to make an error." This sounded so opposed to the Inner Game philosophy that Dorothy thought I was kidding, and she smiled at her next error.

"I mean it," I said with unusual authority. "You can see the ball, you can feel your racket, the net is there, the court is there. There's no reason to make an error!" I was surprised by my words, but at the same time I knew they were true. This time Dorothy believed me, and she didn't make a single error for five minutes.

Afterwards, Dorothy asked, "Whatever happened to all that nice, nonjudgmental, let-it-happen stuff?"

"Nice, nonjudgmental, let-it-happen stuff is one-half of the Inner Game of tennis," I answered. "The other half is that there is no need to make an error. It's okay to make errors; there is no need to make errors. No judgment, no mind, no thought, no need for errors. You will make more errors, I will make more errors. That's okay. There is no need to make errors. Do you understand the two sides? They really fit together perfectly. *Let it happen* is one side; *be totally aware* is the other. 'It's okay to make errors' is one side; 'there is no need for a single error' is the other. We must have both sides." I had never spoken quite like that. It was as if Self 1 was listening to Self 2 say what it had known all along.

After this incident I found myself wanting to be less indulgent with errors and their mental causes. But playing tennis by the usual scoring system didn't tell me whether I was making more or less errors, so I devised a scoring system that would. Here it is.

At the end of every point, the loser declares whether he missed because of an outright error (a shot easily within his capability), a forced error (a shot that was difficult to return, but still within his capability) or an outright winner (a shot beyond his present capacity to return). For an outright error the loser receives a -1 score and the winner is awarded 0 because he didn't earn anything. For a forced error the loser earns a $-1/2$ point and the winner a $+1/2$. For an outright winner the loser's score is unchanged and the winner receives $+1$. Normally I play twenty points to a set, with each player serving five points in a row.

There are additional subtleties that can be introduced into this system, but the principle is clear. Such a scoring system better represents how a player is doing against his own Self 1 mind—the inner opponent—as well as how he scores against his outer opponent. For instance, if after twenty points the score is -6 to -7, it is clear that both players had trouble with their minds. But if the same individuals were to win $+3$ to $+2$ it is obvious there were relatively few outright errors and a higher percentage of winners and forced errors on both sides. A $+11$ to $+9$ score would be possible if neither player made an error.

There is one further complication to the scoring system which can be introduced to encourage consistency. The players can mutually agree that after a certain number of returned balls they each are automatically awarded $+1$ point. If a beginner is playing someone more experienced, they might decide that the former would receive $+1$ for returning at least three balls consecutively, while the latter would have to return five. In this way not only is consistency encouraged, but a natural handicap system provides better competition.

Errorless tennis is only a target to shoot for. It is designed as an incentive for one's determination to overcome the inner obstacles which prevent a player from expressing his full potential. It is *not* designed as one more way to judge oneself as "good" or "bad." It helps the player of the Inner Game to remember exactly which game he is really playing.

Strengthening the Will to Win

The preceding pages have dealt with strengthening one's will by clarifying its direction. But once one has decided what game one really wants to play and what winning really is—at least until he sees a better game—he can sustain and even increase the magnitude of his will.

Here are six general guidelines for strengthening your will to win:

1. Increase awareness of where you are—that is, your situation.
2. Increase awareness of where you want to go—that is, of achieving your goal.
3. Let go of internal interferences—fears, self-doubt, concepts.
4. Give up unnecessary objectives.
5. Seek active inspiration from those of like commitment.
6. Practice frequently and with awareness.

Before elaborating on these guidelines, I want to offer one note of caution. That part of you which wants to strengthen its will to win is *only* a part. There are other elements in your make-up which are content with the way things are, and still others which will resist any kind of increase in your determination. This is perfectly natural. Whenever we become determined to reach a goal, only two results are possible. Either we attain the goal or we fail because of strong resistance from within. By encountering and fighting this resistance we come to know ourselves better. We may find that we really didn't desire what we thought we did as badly as we believed. (The strength of one's will can always be measured by the amount of resistance it is willing to overcome or bypass to reach its goal.) Or we may find that the resistance comes from a desire which is really deeper and truer than our original intention. In that case we learn from the experience and begin to steer a truer course. In either case we increase our awareness of what it is we really want and of where we are starting from.

I have deliberately kept the following guidelines general so that they apply to whatever goals one may choose on or off the court.

Knowing Where You Are

Awareness of where you are at any given moment has been the starting point for every Inner Game process discussed. It sounds almost too simple to take seriously, but in fact it is the step most overlooked by players of tennis and of life. There is only one place a person can make an improvement *from,* and that is where he is already at. One has to be willing to be where he now is before going somewhere else. If you try to go to New York and think you are in Florida but actually are in Chicago, you will steer the wrong course. Some players think they are closer to their goals than they really are, and some exaggerate the distance from their goals. Awareness of what is *at this moment* is the essential starting point. The only place to begin is with the backhand, the awkwardness or the concentration that you have right now. If you are eager to change your bad swing, your bad habit or your bad life, but are unwilling to look at them as they are, change will be extremely difficult. Seeing what *is* requires nonjudgmental awareness and interested acceptance in conditions as they are. Accept them, because only then can you see clearly how to reach your objective. Don't be afraid that this recognition will encourage your "bad" habits. Indeed, you will find that the opposite is true: acceptance of an undesired action will decrease the chances of its recurring, whereas, as we have seen on the tennis courts, judging and resisting will usually increase a habit's frequency.

If you can fully accomplish this first step—acceptance of yourself as you are—you will have simultaneously arrived at your basic goal.

Knowing Where You Want to Go

However, the chances are that no matter how nonjudgmentally you look at yourself, it will be impossible to feel that you are fine just the way you are. Though you may realize that it is acceptable at any given moment not to be at your full potential, no doubt you will feel the need for something that will allow you to attain that potential more often and for longer periods. It is this sense that something is missing from our experience of ourselves, that we are somehow incomplete, which gives man his incentive to seek and to find more than what he is experiencing at the moment. Generally that something we are looking for is within us right now, but we simply aren't experiencing it for one reason or another. To reiterate: becoming clear about what one wants is often the greatest difficulty for players of any of life's games. Much time is wasted chasing rewards which in the end the striver discovers weren't what he really wanted at all. Like Skinner's pigeons, we chase symbolic rewards. We create conceptions of what we believe will satisfy us, then pursue them as if they were valid without ever questioning whether what we seek will actually rid us of the incompleteness.

If we pay attention, our life experiences can make us more discriminating about our goals. Perhaps the most crucial determination one can make is whether what one is looking for lies outside or within oneself. Is our inner game played to assist us in attaining external goals, or is our outer game played as a medium for winning our inner game? Is your goal located outside your own body or within? Whichever, it is of crucial importance to be aware enough to tell the difference between what satisfies you and what doesn't. Unconsciousness of self is a waste of time and energy. Any person who believes he knows what he wants and pursues it with awareness will learn from his experience, whatever the results, simply because he won't stay stuck for long in any game which isn't taking him where he really wants to go. If he does get bogged down temporarily, as soon as he frees himself he will play his next game with greater refinement.

Since the foregoing may sound relevant only to the selection of one's ultimate goal, let me give an example from day-to-day life. After dinner one evening I didn't feel like doing the dishes, but there was no one else available, so, bored and restless, I started washing them in the spirit of meeting an obligation. But, facing the fact that the dishes had to be cleaned, I asked myself, What would you rather be doing? My first answer was that I wanted to get out of the kitchen and find a more interesting way to spend my time.

But another voice said, No, someone has to do them, and you're the only one here. So again I asked myself, Well, then, what do you really want? This time the answer was more clear: what I really wanted was to do the dishes, but to enjoy the task in the process. I heard myself saying, "I don't want to do these dishes. It's a drag being a martyr." It's hard to describe what happened next, but this change in attitude made the fifteen minutes in the kitchen an enjoyable experience. I decided that I wanted to wash the dishes with efficiency and love, and soon I was noticing surprising details like the action of soap on food. The process of rinsing and cleaning stimulated intellectual analogies, and I found challenge in doing the job with full awareness of every motion. In fact, it was no longer a job as soon as I focused on what I was doing. The result was that I washed the dishes better than I ever did before, and did them more quickly and with unprecedented enjoyment. My greatest satisfaction came from realizing that I was getting high on a very ordinary task, something which I had always considered a nuisance. Once again it was confirmed to me that when one commits himself to winning the Inner Game, every external situation can be turned to advantage and each one is important.

Of course, I still find it easy to forget what I really want all too frequently, and such mundane activities will again be automatic and wastefully unconscious. But whenever I realize that I am bored or anxious, I will try to ask myself, What do you really want? As I practice this exercise in daily life I cannot help but get closer in a realistic way to knowing what I want in a larger sense. By being aware of what I want in the little things, I approach clarity in the larger questions of what I want in and from life. Conversely, as I acquire an increased sense of my overall purpose as a human being, it in turn becomes easier to answer the question of what I really want in day-to-day situations. And the better I see the connection between my overall purpose and my daily activities, the greater the sense of meaning and the higher the level of interest I will develop. Thus, knowing what you want is a constant process of paying attention to your experiences, both internal and external, and of refining your sense of purpose.

Yet it is probably true that man's deepest yearnings cannot

be put into words or even imagined. If we could put our purpose into concepts, we would so diminish them that they could not possibly satisfy the limitless nature of our longing. If we could ever really imagine what it is we have been looking for, we would already have achieved it—and having won, wouldn't be concerned with the will to win.

Letting Go of Internal Interferences

Overcoming the mental obstacles that prevent one from reaching his goals has been the primary emphasis of this book. The major barriers discussed have been anxiety, self-doubt, boredom, false concepts, the limiting of one's image, unconsciousness, and Self 1's trying too hard. The methods for overcoming each of these barriers are the same: increase your awareness of what is; learn to discriminate between belief and reality; become aware of that part of yourself which is trustworthy and then put your faith in it to take you where you want to go; let go of the judging mind and of trying too hard; never doubt the existence of the potential within you. Awareness is the light which dispels the defeatist nature of all of our self-induced mental obstacles.

Thus, the Inner Game is above all a game of subtraction that attempts not to add qualities to a self conceived to be full of deficiencies, but to free oneself of whatever is preventing the expression of our potential. The possibility of attaining any realistic goal is already within the individual, so the successful player of the Inner Game has only to subtract the obstacles that prevent his inner potential from expressing itself. He does this in the belief that without the encumbrance of his own inner impediments it is far easier to conquer the external obstacles one may face.

Giving Up Unnecessary Objectives

This step concerns the abandonment of desires and projects which sap an individual's time and energy and deflect them from his real goal. It is the sacrificing of unnecessary concepts or habits in the interest of concentrating more energy in a particular direction. Only by making such sacrifices does a player experience the power of dedication. Yet this is one of the hardest exercises for some people to do. Generally we prefer to hang on to the illustration that we can win all our games at once and have all our wishes granted, in spite of the fact that they may be mutually exclusive. For example, a man who wants to be a leader may have to sacrifice his desire to be one of the boys. A woman who wishes to fulfill her unique potential as a musician must sacrifice living up to the expectations of her parents that she become a lawyer. To increase the energy we place on achieving one goal requires sacrificing some other drive. Sometimes we hate the idea of narrowing ourselves, and we tend to dislike commitment and dedication because it seems to limit our alternatives. But this is the nature of the game. Freedom comes only with a willingness to narrow one's objectives; success is attained only when we have been able and willing to put all our energy into our truest purpose. Concentrating our will works exactly the same way as concentrating our attention. To pay attention to one object—say, reading this book—usually requires withdrawing it from another. This is what makes choice a real decision and life a game of infinite variety. The trick is to put one's energies into what one truly wants, rather than to waste one's precious conscious energy on goals which don't give him what he needs.

Most energy is lost in chasing the appearance of our purposes rather than the reality—for example, those tennis players who choose to look good rather than *be* good. But Self 1's desires for a self-image, which is nothing but appearance, can be abandoned in the interest of actually achieving one's potential.

The release of energy which follows the genuine sacrifice of a Self 1 desire is usually awesome. It's happened to me on several occasions which are vivid in my memory. One of these occurred just after I had graduated from college, when I was at a conference of a large number of people, almost none of whom I knew. I had always considered myself shy, and usually felt slightly intimidated by anyone I didn't know well. During the conference, I accepted a challenge to play an "honesty game" of my own choice. I elected to list the specific ways I tried to bluff other people. That is, I wrote down a description of the image that I tried to present to others, and exactly how I did it. Afterwards I had to read what I had written to a group of five others around a table who were strangers. Part of what I confessed was my tendency to try to impress others with my intellectuality by using longer and more abstract words than necessary. Then, having exposed myself, I realized that I couldn't use this bluff any more because it couldn't fool them—or me.

I was surprised that no one seemed greatly affected one way or the other, but treated me in much the same way as when I had been wearing my mask. When I got up from that table, I experienced something astonishing: I felt at home with all the other people at the conference. I had no fear. I knew that any one of them would be interesting to talk to and spend time with. I became aware of a great deal of energy in myself, and that it wanted to express itself to others in a way that I had never felt before. It wasn't until some time later that I realized how much effort is usurped by Self 1's image projects to the detriment of the natural expression of our true potentialities.

In daily life, I find that I have always been most satisfied when I exert my energy fully on whatever I am doing, no matter how unimportant it may seem. This is not easy for me, because my habit is to concentrate only when I think that the task is "important." But in a true perspective every moment is equally important and deserves our full consciousness. Billie Jean King seems to have realized this. When Howard Cosell interviewed her after her stunning victory at Wimbledon in 1975, he asked, "What did you do to get yourself up for this match? Did you wake up in the morning and strangle a few chickens?" Billie Jean's patient reply was, "No, I woke up, and everything I did thereafter I put myself fully into. Then I just kept doing the same thing out on the court, and I played out of my mind!"

One more remark on the sacrifice of conflicting or distracting desires: do it gently. *Kiss* them goodbye when you become aware that the goal isn't really what you want, or that you don't want it as much as something else. Otherwise the desires will continue to haunt you, and the distraction will keep you from reaching your primary goal.

How does one sacrifice? There are three basic methods:

1. By *perceiving* that a particular desire isn't really what one wants. Then it departs automatically.
2. By starving the desire—that is, simply not acting on its behalf. If it isn't strong, it will weaken if you refuse to feed it.
3. By fulfilling it. If it keeps recurring and prevents you from reaching your goal, you can choose to confront the desire by fulfilling it and then seeing whether or not it's what you really wanted.

To reiterate: our experience is what teaches us.

Active Inspiration from Those of Like Commitment

Once a player has decided on his goal and dedicated himself to it, his will to reach it can be strengthened by keeping the company of people of like commitment. Our will needs to be inspired to stay consistently strong, and that inspiration comes best from those who are genuinely committed to the same objective. If a bank robber "hangs out" with other enthusiastic and competent bank robbers, he will be inspired by their dedication and will learn from their experience. Likewise, when dedicated tennis players get together they increase each other's understanding of the game, and by competing challenge one another to expend the effort necessary to reach the limits of their potential. Just by talking with other players who love the game and by watching good tennis, one's will to continue and enjoyment of practice increase. Those who play the inner game of life benefit in the same way by sharing dedication and experience with those of similar commitment. To travel alone is a difficult way to play any game.

Practicing Frequently and with Awareness

All the awareness, sacrifice and inspiration in the world will achieve nothing if a player does not practice his game. When you want to do something well, there is no substitute for doing it often. Of course, everybody practices the game he prefers, but if the practice is to be beneficial, he has to be conscious. If you hit a million balls against a backboard, and are inattentive or bored, your arm may grow stronger, but your awareness won't, and little will be learned; in fact, you may not even recognize that you're bored and playing a game you don't enjoy.

The single greatest strengthener of one's will is to complete an action or project in the name of that will. Conversely, to talk about intentions without acting on them is perhaps the greatest saboteur of one's will. Talking about tennis without practicing it gives the player only the illusion that he is learning the game. Talking about truth without practicing it leads the seeker away from his goal. (I speak from experience; the greatest weakener of the will of an author to complete his book is to substitute talking about it for doing it. The talk is easy, and it saps perseverance.)

Talking about love is no substitute for loving, and discussing what's wrong with one's life goals is an easy way to dispel the energy necessary to change those goals. Only by taking action on our intentions can we really strengthen them and learn if they are valid. All progress comes only from experience, and the more conscious the experience, the more one benefits.

Likewise, one learns concentration of mind only by attempting it, and it is a skill which can be practiced at all moments of one's life, no matter what else one is doing. Playing the Inner Game to overcome the limitations of one's mind is not a philosophy, but a *practice,* and its "theories" are nothing more than descriptions of the pragmatic results I have experienced while evolving the Inner Game. The validity of these exercises can really only be tested by practicing and seeing for yourself.

In short, this is a plea that you not substitute believing in the Inner Game for doing it—or, for that matter, that you not substitute any beliefs, including those espoused in these pages, for the knowledge that comes from direct experience.

8
On Winning
the Inner Game

A player's awareness of the Inner Game usually passes
through several stages. First he becomes aware that he is in
it; next he comes to the understanding that it is worth playing; then he plays it consciously while looking for better ways
to progress. In the last step he comes to a realization of what
winning the Inner Game means, and thereafter may devote
his will to arriving at nothing short of that goal.

Generally people discover the existence of the Inner Game
at a point when they do not truly comprehend that it is
primarily internal obstacles, not external ones, which are
preventing them from reaching their objective. This discovery can be made not only on the tennis court but in any
arena, and for most people it is an understanding which
transforms their perspective on what their lives are all about
and how to live them. But the incentive to play the Inner
Game consciously usually only comes when the individual
has experienced in a practical way the benefits of quieting the
mind a little, of discovering and letting go at least some of
the limitations he has imposed on himself. As these obstacles
are partially or momentarily withdrawn, the novice player
discovers some of his true capabilities. The more he frees